John Hugh McNaughton

Onnalinda

A Romance

John Hugh McNaughton

Onnalinda
A Romance

ISBN/EAN: 9783744770408

Printed in Europe, USA, Canada, Australia, Japan

Cover: Foto ©ninafisch / pixelio.de

More available books at **www.hansebooks.com**

ONNALINDA

ONNALINDA

A ROMANCE

BY

J. H. McNAUGHTON

If I could write the beauty of your eyes,
And in fresh numbers number ALL your graces,
The age to come would say, this poet lies—
Such heavenly touches ne'er touched earthly faces
SHAKSPEARE

Illustrated

LONDON
KEGAN PAUL, TRENCH & CO., 1 PATERNOSTER SQ.

NEW YORK
ONNALINDA PUBLISHING CO., 27 UNION SQ.

1888

PRINTED BY FRANK WOOD, BOSTON.

History is vague and legendary concerning the achievements of ONNALINDA, the Iroquois princess, whose brilliant adroitness baffled the French general Denonville in his invasion of her father's domains; and whose fascinating beauty drew to her side, from the ranks of her enemies, the chivalrous Captain Stark. The loves and adventures of the gallant captain and the charming Onnalinda, together with the story of Ronald Kent and "Glinting Star," are in the province of ROMANCE, and the theme of this tale.

ILLUSTRATIONS
engraved by
FRANK FRENCH
From Drawings
By
WILLIAM T. SMEDLEY
1886.

PRINTED BY
FRANK WOOD, BOSTON.

LIST OF ILLUSTRATIONS.

IN THE FOREST: ALONE, - - - - Frontispiece.

> "One hand to ear to catch alarm
> Showed jeweled wrist and rounded arm."

HEADPIECE TO PART I. - - - - - Page 1

> "A lordly castle, broad and high,
> Was home of her nativity."

A SUDDEN INTRUSION, - - - - - " 34

> "They halted by my covert near . . . .
> My heart seemed throbbing in my ear."

THE TRIO: TO THE RENDEZVOUS, - - - " 54

> "By her side the chieftain dark,
> And on her right, proud Eben Stark."

THE BURNING SHIP, - - - - - 72

> "A wreck! A wreck! — Shoremen ahoy —
> She's plunging for the land!"

MOONLIGHT INTERVIEW, - - - - - " 82

> "Her white arm round a moonlit tree
> Glistened with jeweled brilliancy."

THE IMPASSIONED HEROINE, - - - - " 106

> "Flashed her black eyes with fire of scorn,
> And warriors quailed with look forlorn."

HEADPIECE TO PART II, - - - - - Page 109

"And by the campfire's flickering light."

A SIGNAL ACHIEVEMENT, - - - - - " 118

"Swift as the shimmering swallow-flight
She pierced the waves athwart the night."

THE HEROINE'S STRATAGEM, - - - - " 138

"The craggy steep dim-lit with glow
Of lurid campfire from below."

PERSONS REPRESENTED.

ONNALINDA, *the Iroquois princess who both fascinated and disconcerted her enemies.*

KAWANUTE, *father of Onnalinda and chieftain of the Iroquois, whose country was invaded by the French under the Marquis Denonville.*

EBEN STARK, *an English captain who had joined the French, but, captivated by the charms of the Princess, abandoned the Marquis.*

RONALD KENT, *the marksman of marvellous aim, and comrade of Captain Stark — in love with Glinting Star.*

GLINTING STAR, *daughter of an Algonquin chief.*

OONAK, *the silent — the Judas of the red race.*

DENONVILLE'S COURIER, *a punctilious Frenchman.*

OSSEOLO, *an unhappy lover of Onnalinda.*

DONALD, *a facetious Scot.*

SCENE: *mainly in the valley of the Genesee during its invasion by the French.*

ONNALINDA

Part I

She by descent from royal lineage came
Of ancient kings and queens, that had of yore
Their sceptres stretched from east to western shore.

FAERIE QUEENE, Book I.

ONNALINDA.

—

Part I

I

In the Forest. Alone.

Alone she stood, a maiden sweet,
  Within the woodland's deepening shade;
  One beam of sunset through the glade
Glimmered in gold about her feet.
  Musing, she lingered in covert there,
Far from the clamour of camp's alarms;
Above her a beech flung out his arms
  As if to shield a form so fair.

1

Near her a brook in jocund glee
Leapt chattering down to the Genesee.

II

A winsome girl of native grace
    And moulded form the comeliest;
    Scarce two-and-twenty Junes had kiss'd
With breath of rose her charming face—
    Brunette, with crimson tinged and blent,
As if 'neath Saxon face there glowed
The warm maroon of Indian blood,
    And stirred a doubt of her descent—
A doubt that still intenser grew
With her rich garb of Tyrian hue.
Her queenly grace and soft attire
Bespoke a line from noble sire.

Around her bodice trimly laced
    Fell glossy falls of her raven hair,
    Half veiling, half revealing there
The zone that clasped her lissome waist.

    One hand to ear, to catch alarm,
    Showed jewelled wrist and rounded arm.

In purple folds her kirtle fell —
 The rimpling hem just kissed her feet,
 In shoon of chamois fitted neat
As glove and palm of courtly belle;
 Beneath her instep, proud and high,
 A flower would bloom, a bee would fly.

The charms of youth and beauty met
In ONNALINDA — sweet brunette!

III

In a lonely nook why lingered she?
 Tho' on the ground her eyes were bent,
 A glance afar she frequent sent
As if in pleased expectancy.

Deep in her dark eyes' lustrous glance
Glistened the star of bright Romance.

She listened. . . .

          Silent all the wood
 Save plaintive owl, in distant glade,
 Whose croon, thro' echoing forest, made
More solemn still the solitude.

Then to herself the maiden spoke—
　　Still gazing pensive on the ground
　　As if perplexed with thoughts profound—
And murmuring, thus the silence broke:

"Last night—what did he mean to say?
　　My hand in his he tremulous prest;
　　I heard a throbbing within his breast:
'Good-bye,' he faltered, and turned away,—
　　But in his voice and in his eye
　　Was something more than that 'Good-bye.'

"The white moon shone on his earnest face
　　As he held my hand, and silent stood.
　　Do men woo thus in a dolesome mood?
Then a solemn owl may woo with grace!
　　This man—can he be my father's foe
　　And lover of mine? To-night I'll know:

"To-night when the moon shines full in his face
　　I'll there read clear each thought of his heart;
　　He shall not know, as I stand apart,
How keen my glance each line shall trace.
　　Ah, well, my heart! do I love this man—
　　So soon? Perchance I do—or can."

She paused. Around she gazed, and then,
Musing, she spoke to herself again:

"What if my chieftain-sire should know—
    Should know I parley with foe of his!
    Well, what if I foil his enemies
  With weapon keener than blade or bow?
    Perchance this Saxon loves me well. . .
    Sink low, O sun!—to-night will tell."

    Once more she paused, and to and fro
    In revery moved, repeating low
  "Perchance this Saxon loves me well. . . .
    Sink low, O sun!—TO-NIGHT will tell."

IV

The sun behind the glimmering hill
    His amber lances slow withdrew,
    And twilight shadows a glamour threw
Around the woodlands soft and still.
    A crackling sound beyond the glade
Reached Onnalinda's vigilant ear;
Then startled owl thrid by anear,
    Flapping across the forest shade.

Quicker her heart beat at each sound—
Silence and darkness gathering round.

Sudden she turned. A rustling tread
  She heard approach thro' the darkling wood.
  Flushed to the ear, alert she stood,
'Twixt hope and fear disquieted.
Soon thro' the woodland tripping light
  Came footsteps she was wont to hear;
  No form she saw, but to her ear
That sound was palpable as sight:
If woman hear, what need to see?
One step she knows intuitively!

V

A manly form with cap of blue
  Approached. His epauletted coat,
  Bright-buttoned trimly to his throat,
Of rank and fame was symbol true.
But more his eye and bearing told
  Than any sign symbolic could;
  (Escutcheons mark the noble blood,
But mien and port the noble-souled;)

Needing no badge nor gilded mace—
Chivalric honour in his face.

O'er log and limb he supple springs
   With form erect; his visage bright
   With azure eyes; his beard of night
Above his lips like raven wings.
    Heroic calmness in his face
    Showed valour 'neath a gentle grace.

VI

THE COLLOQUY.

"Brief be our words to-night,"—he said,
   As her warm hand in his he drew;
   His words, foreboding, o'er her threw
Shadows of some impending dread;—
"But start not, Onnalinda sweet!
Though swift I come, on hurrying feet,
Through rustling brake and forest dim
With greetings in an anxious tone,—
No harm betides thee, gentle one.
And yet, if rumour tricks me not,
Alert with stratagem and plot

The midnight hour shall be.
My wary scout from yonder hill
Saw hurried signals that reveal
Some tumult rife that bodes of ill—
    Some pending strategy:
Thy chieftain-sire, brave Kawanute,
And warriors of moccas'ined foot
Are gathering swift from hunt and chase
At Rounded Cove, the mustering place."

"Such signals"—Onnalinda said—
    "May oftentimes foreshadow ill,
    But oft, to try their speed and skill,
'Mong warriors false alarms are spread,
    As fawn is bred to flee from harm
    When stamps the doe a false alarm—
Thus wary is the warrior bred.
My clan the Saxon's art would meet
With weasel's eye and fox's feet!
Perchance—alas!—there's peril near;
Perchance 't is death to linger here!"

HE.

No fear the Saxon warriors know
Of lurking spy or open foe.

One fear alone the bravest feel
Keener than lance of bristling steel:
'Neath one bright glance of Beauty's eye
They quail submissive—pine, and sigh!
What if deep plots are lurking laid
To tangle the feet in ambuscade?
We smile at such—at snare or threat—
But quail 'neath glance of bright brunette!
—— But say, when from the camp you came
Where were the warriors?

ONNALINDA.

Hunting game.

HE.

And of those warriors, is there none
Watching your footsteps?

ONNALINDA.

There is one.

HE.

One—who is he?

ONNALINDA.

A warrior, brave,
But silent as a forest grave.
2

"And therefore to be feared?"—said he.
"I know not,"—crimsoning, said she,
And smiled as if her words revealed
But inkling of the thoughts concealed.

VII

Silent he stood, with downcast eyes;
A sudden doubt his heart oppressed,
Like one who sees, low in the west,
Dark clouds that threaten the sunny skies.
"I know not."—In her words a doubt—
A dim surmise and mystery—
That roused the phantom Jealousy,
A shadow Love is never without.

And as she spoke, a glance she sent
Oblique across the forest glade,
And turned an ear as if intent
On distant sound from ambuscade.
Heard she a signal?—was it meant
For friend, or foe—for man, or maid?
No heed gave *he;* another theme
In heart and brain now reigned supreme.

Touched deep with a mysterious sting
 At Onnalinda's words of doubt,
 He strove adroit to draw her out —
Feigning a careless questioning:
"Perchance this warrior's silent tongue
Tattled and prattled gay, when *young?*"

ONNALINDA.

Who talks the least I call him wise —
Words are but dust thrown in the eyes.

HE.

Then far the wisest you would call
A sphinx who will not talk at all,
Or talks in tropes equivocal.

ONNALINDA.

No, yes, and no. I've heard him say:
"The wise man mingles yea and nay —
At once both nods and shakes his head "—
So . . . so the silent warrior said.

HE.

Such wisdom comes with veteran age,—
Is he your tribal seer and sage?

ONNALINDA.

Age but a test or proof supplies—
The fools *grow* foolish; the wise more wise.

VIII

About the pretty bush he beat,
  But stirred no quarry in his quest;
The bird, to lure the hunter's feet,
  Ranged, fluttering, round her hidden nest.
So Onnalinda, bright and shrewd,
Would Eben's anxious quest elude:
She answers wise-obscure, and thus
He gropes in phrase ambiguous.

He feared to ask her, frank and fair,
  Of him who stirred his jealousy—
  Ashamed to ask: "A lover, he?"—
He hunted here, he angled there,
With fisher's hook but ill-concealed—
The point was through the bait revealed!

Undaunted still he questioned her
  With ill-disguised anxiety;

And still as archly answered she
With flowery trope and fallacy—
The shrewd, the charming sophister!

HE.

Young Indian warrior, we are told,
Makes hasty' wooing, brief and bold.

ONNALINDA.

Nimble his pace in love or chase,
And both his eyes are in his face; *
I 'm told a pale-face in canoe
Will one way look, another go—
Will eastward face, and westward row!

HE.

I see . . . you think when Saxons woo
They feign one thing, and another do?

ONNALINDA.

Has he two tongues? So said my mother;
He woos one maid and wins another;

---

* " Mr. Facing-both-ways, Mr. Two-Tongues . . . was but
a waterman, looking one way and rowing another."— BUNYAN.

To that one throws a mimic kiss
To kindle jealous love in this;
Flirting with blonde to win the brown:
Like fire-brand in one dwelling thrown
To burn another in the town!

HE.

Your "mother" said?—How could she know?

ONNALINDA.

Not forest-born was she—no, no;
Her eye was blue, her brow was snow.

HE.

A Saxon, she?

ONNALINDA.

                    Sweet face, so fair!

HE.

Then like . . . like thee?

ONNALINDA.

                    As well compare
A murky torch to her—a star
Shining among the Blest Afar.

HE.

Then a lovely woodland nymph was she,—
Not forest born?

ONNALINDA.

From o'er the sea,—
Where blooming hedge-rows carolled sweet,
And heather blossomed 'neath her feet.
At quiet eve she oft would tell
Of scenes enchanting, and would dwell
With trembling lip, and tenderly,
On home beloved, beyond the sea;
Of twilight porch, with ivy pent;
Of castle wall and battlement;
Of arch antique and turret high,
And gilded spires that lanced the sky;
Of tender lawn in bright demesne
Soft as the velvet shoon of queen;
Of gateway whence of old there went
Knights to the joust and tournament.
. . . You wonder? Sir, I pardon you—
The tale *is* strange.

HE.

I'd swear 't is true,—

A myth for truth I would admit
When lips so sweet have uttered it!
Bright as the tale of chivalry!
  To-night I 'll dream of all things fair:
  Of looming castles in the air,
Of lords and ladies of high degree,
  Of stately halls and gilded rooms
  Sweet-scented with the heather-blooms,—
A charming tale: a fantasy?

ONNALINDA.

Is it so strange a woodland girl
Should claim a grandsire in an earl?

HE.

I know a woodland nymph so sweet
An earl would meekly kiss her feet!
Worthy to grace a royal reign
With forty earls to bear her train!

ONNALINDA.

A Saxon maid?

HE.

                I cannot say
Whether a Saxon, Gaul, or Gael;
She is not dark, she is not pale,

Soft twilight—neither night nor day—
Tinged with the blush of evening sky,
Vermeil and pearl in rivalry;
As if 'neath Saxon's cheek there glowed
The warm maroon of Indian blood.

[He paused. She smiled at his device.
Then added he from "Paradise":]
" Her cheek's soft tincture, even the brain
Shall trace so fine a tint in vain."

ONNALINDA.

Truly, a lovely girl is she!
My mother oft was wont to tell
Of one like her you paint so well,
Beloved by bard of Italy.
—But listen . . . Hark!—do you not hear
Sounds of alarm, of peril near?

HE.

I heed it not, (some wandering breeze
Wailing its sorrow to the trees,)
I hear, I see but mysteries:
Shuttled, as warp with woof, I see
Simplicity with complexity!

Your life's enigma, or I err,
Needs an expert interpreter.
These solitudes have ne'er before
Listened to mediæval lore.

ONNALINDA.

You err. Sweet was its echoing
With songs my mother used to sing.
She sang Torquato's tender lay
    Of him who at the stake had died
    To challenge Death, and win his bride—
The matchless maid Sofronia.
    She told me tales of Greece and Rome;
She sung of Goth and Norman king;
But most she loved—ah! loved to sing
    Sweet Gaelic songs of highland home!
And in that castle, high and broad,
One little room, a bright abode,—
Books, music, pictures—radiant room!—
Sweet with the scent of heather-bloom.

IX

Deeper and darker his suspense,
Shrouded in mist and doubt intense.

As veil that falls o'er Beauty's eyes
  Brightens their charms, tho' half concealed,
The web she wove of words and sighs
  Charmed him with thoughts but half revealed.
A mystery hid in mysteries:
  Why roamed this nymph in solitude,
  Hid in the gloom of pathless wood?
Like jewel in unfathomed seas!
  Still dauntless he, and ardent yet
  To trace this mystic anchoret.
  As the young wren oft lifts its wing—
  To fly from nest oft threatening—
  Vexed with restraint, and braving fate,
  At last it darts precipitate;
  So *he*, impatient of restraint,
  Of thwarted scheme and hope deferred,
  Restive and bolder, like the bird
  He darted forth precipitant
  With winged words; their force direct
  Her shield of wit could not deflect:

"Whence came your mother—when and why?
    You speak of home beyond the sea
    And hedge-rows—all is mystery.
  Forgive me if I urge reply."

Then Onnalinda answered shrewd:
"What if 't is true a woodland girl
    Shall claim a grandsire in an earl
Of proud manorial habitude?
Armorial signs will not gainsay—
    Of title the unerring guide;
    And now your shrewdness shall decide
His rank by his insignia,—
'T is thus: Upon his coronet
The leaves *above* the pearls are set."

X

A SIGNAL.

Awhile deep musing, mute stood he—
    Like baffled general in assault
    When fortress-moat compels a halt
To compass the emergency—
When—hark!—upon his watchful ear
    A sound from far. Not loud halloo,
    But such as wary hunters blow
'Twixt thumbs—a whistle low, but clear;
A sound the wanderer to direct,
Or signal to be circumspect—
A vigilant tone, as if 't were blown
Subdued, for watchful ear alone.

And hark! again—that sound renewed,
Louder, and echoing thro' the wood.

XI

"Dear one! I go,"—he anxious said.—
"On wings how fleet has evening fled!
Once more I ask that pledge so dear:
To-morrow eve to meet me here."

"If stars be bright—if woods be still—
If signals no alarm reveal—
If nought doth wake the jealous eye,
To-morrow night," . . . was her reply.

Her hand upon his lips he pressed
Tenderly, saying: "O sweet good-night!"
They parted. Dim the stars' pale light.
His heart beat with a strange unrest,
Murmuring: "Can such bliss be mine?
Or is she hidden in dark design?"

As through the darkling wood he went,
The phantom Doubt danced in his way;
With twit and taunt it seemed to say
With a goblin's mocking merriment:

"IF stars be bright! IF woods be still!
  If, if she won't—if, if she will!
    See bats at noon, and linnets at dark,
    Then trust a Beauty, O Eben Stark!"

And visions rose before him then
  In dark ravine and gruesome lair;
Fantastic voices from the glen
  Shrilled ominous:
                "Beware! Beware!—
To-morrow night a shadow dark
Shall cross the glade, O Eben Stark!"

XII

Through shadowy paths of woodland dim
  Regretful Eben went his way;
  As jocund elves in prank and play,
So frolicked Love and Doubt with him!

But thrice ere this had Eben met
  Sweet Onnalinda at the tryst,—
  Did love thrive slow? He had but kissed
The rosy points of her fingers yet.

Dare he not look up from her finger-tips
To the opulent curve of her crimson lips?

Thrice met; and lovelier than before
Sparkled her eyes of glistening dew:
Thrice met; and more enchanting grew
A form Apelles might adore.

And Eben's heart beat wild and fast,
Thrilled with the touch of her finger-tips
That tingled still on his quivering lips
As thro' the crackling wood he passed.
And vexed was he at a signal sent
Thwarting his passionate heart's attent.

———

(Thrice had they met—the Muse hath told—
But how they met at first by chance,
A prelude strange to Love's romance,
The sequel fitter will unfold
In words of hers—from lips that give
A witchery to her narrative;
And whence came Eben, why, and when,
Will serve the tale and Eben then.)

There Onnalinda lingered yet
  Within the starlit nook alone;
  Ah! yielding heart—and will it own
One tender sigh for the man she met?
.. "O peaceful night!—so calm,"—she said—
"Why is my heart disquieted?
O happy bird with folded wing,
  Would that thy peace were mine!"—she sighed.
  In quavering tones she, faltering, tried
This tender woodland song to sing:

ONNALINDA'S SONG.

Why art thou calm, O peaceful night!
  While in my heart a wild unrest?
And thou, O star! why beam so bright,
  While dark my heart with doubt opprest?
      O star of night!
      I turn to thee;
      O calm, calm night,
      Bring calm to me!

O balmy breeze! with breath of spring
  Breathe thy soft murmurs in my ear;
And thou, sweet bird! awake and sing
  That song a maiden loves to hear.
      Sweet bird! O sing
      My heart to rest,
      Then fold thy wing
      In happy nest!

As one would sing whose thought and tongue
Held themes diverse, she, musing, sung.
Then from the nook she slow withdrew.
    Along the river her pathway led.

" Flow on, O river, in peace,"—she said—
" Would that my path were peaceful too:
    Across my way is drawn a bar,—
    Who is this man who comes from far ?"

XIII

Wherefore did Onnalinda sigh ?
    Was it o'er Eben's "sweet good-night"?
    Was it for dusky forest-wight —
Perchance that silent warrior ?—why ?

Perchance for both ?—or neither !— vexed
    Like traveller where his road divides,
    In wavering doubt till he decides,—
Was Onnalinda thus perplexed ?

Meek but adroit—ah ! who can tell
Beauty's intent inscrutable !

XIV

A LURKING FORM.

She neared her home thro' winding ways.
  Far into night the hours had fled.
  The camp-fires smouldered murky red,
Save one that darted tongues ablaze—
  Tingeing the glen with baleful light,
  And reddening far the shades of night.

With fagots fresh what sleepless one
  Had roused to flame that quickened fire?
  Was one awake with jealous ire—
With keen suspicion restive grown?

Was there a lurking form that stood
Back in the darkness of the wood?

Slumbered her sire. No thought he gave
  Mistrustful of the absent one:
  He knew her wont to wander alone
And linger beside her mother's grave;
  In sylvan glade a mound of green
  'Neath hallowed moonlight slept serene.

Often beneath the starry sky
  Her gentle footsteps thither led,
  And softly over the sainted dead
Her dirge would blend with breeze's sigh.

Nay—'t was not he—her slumbering sire,—
  Another's hand that fagot lit
  As sign and symbol that like it
Flamed jealous love with deathless fire!

  Suspicion steals from harassed bed,
  And tiptoe glides with stealthy tread.

But Onnalinda, light and fleet,
  Skipt noiseless, bird-like, to her nest,
  Folded her winged thoughts to rest
With saintlier prayer from lips so sweet.

Her drooping lashes fell and rose
  Like leaf when breathes soft evening's balm:
  They fall; they rise; now drooping calm,
Softly upon her cheek repose.
  Leave her to dream.
                Afar we speed
  To yonder wood across the mead.

XV

A COURIER.

"*Halloo?*" a voice from jungle cried.

"Halloo!" quick Eben Stark replied.

(We follow Eben's supple feet
Alert his sentry's call to meet.)

It sounds again thro' forest dark,
　The sentry's call—and low, subdued,
　And lower yet as thro' the wood
Nearer it came to Eben Stark.

"Halloo?"—

　　　　"Halloo!" came the reply.

EBEN.

Well, Ronald, what 's the stir, and why?

RONALD.

A courier from the Frenchman came.

EBEN.

A scout from Denonville?

RONALD.
　　　　　　The same.

He's at our camp—he waits for you.

EBEN.

Confound his dastard "parlez vous"!
  I'm done with war. I'm done with raid.
  I'm done with sneaking ambuscade—
I'm now for—

RONALD.

  Pretty Indian maid!

EBEN.

Whisht! Ronald,—you're a canny Scot,
But winds may blow that whistle not!

———

Ronald, a Scot—young, lithe, and brave,
  With honour's face and eagle's eye;
  Ready at quip's hilarity,
But timely resolute, and grave.

Of cultured brain, yet often he
  His lore would clothe in humour brusque—
  Hiding the grain within the husk—
Scorning a show of pedantry.

He and the captain, with a score
　Of knights as chivalrous as they,
　Had listless joined the base foray—
Ignoble deed they now deplore.
　　Ignoble?—Diabolic, base:
　　Slaying for what? A tinge of face!

At morn they view a blooming vale
　Smiling before the hordes of France;
　At eve a scowling, dark expanse—
A blackened land of woe and wail:
War's whirlwind, red with sword and fire,
　Had left but ashes in its path,—
　Hamlets and homes in fiery scath
Swept flaming into ruin dire.

　(A power more potent still than these
　　Drew them aloof from wreck and raid:
　　On Eben's heart a wild crusade
　Was waged by Love's perplexities!—
　　Ah! Love and Doubt—in mingled feud,
　　Like chafing boughs in stormy wood.)

Forth went the twain. Thro' forest dark
　Campward they groped their tangled way;

In wise debate, or jesting gay,
Went Ronald Kent and Captain Stark.

Tho' Ronald oft would chaff and jest,
A look demure would oft suggest
A thorn within his manly breast:
His tenderness it was his wont
To hide with sayings bold or blunt;
Tho' sad of heart, yet often he
Disguised his grief in repartee.

(This thorn that Ronald would conceal
The tale shall by and by reveal.)

EDEN.

What message from the French?

RONALD.

To tramp,
So I suspect. But at the camp
You 'll read it soon. He could but speak
A Gascon gibberish, or Greek.
I winked at Donald and at Aleck
To try him wi' a spurt o' Gaelic.

" *Vail Gaelic agad?*" *—Donald said,
But puzzled Frenchman shook his head.

EBEN.

Gallic, not Gaelic, is his talk —
A Gaul, not Gael, his parent stock.
What is he like?

RONALD.

A Frenchman, sooth!
With two legs only, and a mouth —
The man for an emergency! —
Swift runner and a talker he.

EBEN.

Jesting aside,— his urgency
Betokens ill for you and me.
But soon base Denonville shall know
I was his friend — I am his foe.
He comes with servile hordes at hire
To scathe with sword, and blast with fire
This blooming vale of the Genesee,
Lovely as dell in Arcady!

* Bheil gaidhelig agad,

He comes with Gascons proud and base
To whelm a knightlier, nobler race
Of line antique, of high descent —
The Roman of the Occident.
They call him "savage,"— let them tell
Who crucified IMMANUEL.

RONALD.

And "treacherous," too! Is 't their belief
That Judas was an Indian chief?
We speak of "treachery"! Who begot
The traitor-chief, Iscariot?
And he who first a brother slew —
Was Cain, like Judas, Indian too?
Soon shall we hear — of all things human! —
The serpent was an Indian woman,
And all the woes of earth came in
Slipshod on beaded moccasin!

XVI

They neared an opening in the wood;
  Above the trees the moon arose;
  A bright retreat in soft repose,
Never profaned with raid or feud.

They halt: To Eben seemed so bright
   The glinting nook with dewy glim;
   For all things pure and sweet, to him
Were emblems now of all delight!

And moon, or star, or glistening dew,
   Or breath of June, or song of bird,
(Of Onnalinda emblems true!)
   With rapture all his pulses stirred.

"Love-haunted nook!"—broke Eben thus—
"The dreamy grot of Tityrus!
   There's but one nook on earth like this—
Bright as the eye of Loveliness!"

And Ronald, smiling, shrewdly guessed
Where lay that covert bright and blest;
   And humoring Eben's sentiment,
Thus archly spoke as forth they went:

"Captain! a lovelier nook I know:
One day we chased a wearied doe,
   And thro' that nook with jaded bound
It went, pursued by eager hound.*

* This incident, which led to the first meeting of Onnalinda
and Captain Stark, is dwelt upon, in the sequel, by the heroine
herself.

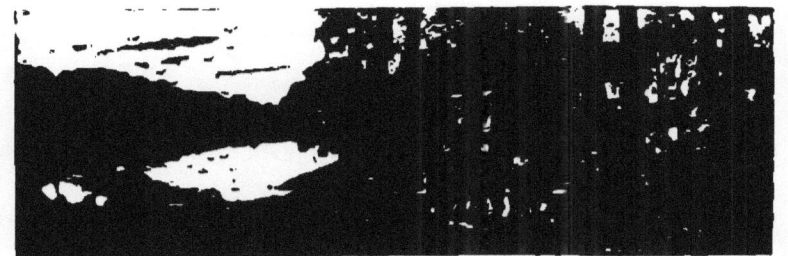

'T was by the river, and the doe
Into it leaped from howling foe."

EBEN.

Ah! Ronald Kent — there first I found
What makes my stormy pulses bound!
From bower secluded forth there came
Who touched my torpid life with flame!
Bright as a star o'er night serene
Smiled ONNALINDA — woodland queen!

RONALD.

Eh? Captain! you 'll be poet soon!

EBEN.

She 'll make a laureate of a loon!

RONALD.

Then I 'll be laureate, and play
Your woodland queen sweet roundelay:
With poet's pibroch sing that she is
Brighter and sweeter than Chryseïs; *

* "A maid, unmatched in manners as in face,
Skill'd in each art, and crown'd with every grace."
                                        —ILIAD, Book I.

With odes that drown the Gascon drum
I 'll strike Olympic Pindar dumb,
Sounding your epithalamium!
Sonnets I 'll scribble, spondees whine,
And stride a butt of Malmsey wine —
From loon to laureate! Oh, the bliss
Of such a metamorphosis! —
. . . But see! a light — the camp is near.

EBEN.

Cease, then, your jest — no trifling here.
The crafty Frenchman we must meet
With craft as subtle and discreet, —
Whate'er his scheme or message, we
Must compass it with strategy, ·
And show this scout from Denonville
That there 's a wheel within a wheel!
. . . Haste, Ronald, haste before, and say
The captain comes — is on his way;
Feign breathless haste, with nostril spread,
As if 't was all for France you sped —
Deceit is never a sin in war —
Treat courier as ambassador.
Go! feign submissive fealty,
And, hark! send Donald out to me.

XVII

SHOW HIM THE LINES!

Forth Ronald hurried to the tent;
  Rushed in as if from jaded bout;
  Made his devoir; sent Donald out;
Then told of risks he underwent:
"The woods are rife with skulking foes —
Dark forms with tomahawks and bows;
Their arrows whizzed, and hatchets spun
As swift as I the gauntlet run!
Thro' forest wild with whoop and howl
Gaunt wolf and dusky savage prowl;
Ambush and snare lurk in the way,—
But duty calls, and I obey.
I count it all a bright romance
And all for glory: 'la belle' France!"

This courier seemed a man of note,
  But polished to a vain excess;
  An exquisite in form and dress,
And sleek in manners as his coat —
  Trim coat! it seemed in form and fit
  Not made for him but he for it,

As if from first he grew within
Like pulp in a banana skin!
He bowed with such consummate grace,
'T was art profound! By slow degrees
'T was perfected through centuries
Of bowing by his polished race.
With jewelled hand, and dainty wrist,
His sleek mustache he 'd twirl and twist;
So exquisite his gay cravat,
His envious chin was wroth with that,
And rose in air with high regard
And pride of the camelopard!
Thus lordly he — of lofty port —
As envoy from barbaric court.

"Ho — bien!" exclaimed the Frenchman. He
  Through fog of Ronald's words could see
"Glory" and "France." The rest was dim —
  Just vague enough to harry him;
  Tho' leal and true he deemed these men,
  He feared his pathway home again!
  For Ronald's feint of terror showed
  Perils abroad the night forebode, —
  As spectres in the twilight dim
  Seem swelling huge, and ghostly grim,

So, words the Frenchman knew not well
Swelled phantom-like more terrible:
Tho' vexed with words of shadowy sense
He feigned a cool indifference;
But through his guise they well could see
The courier's vexed anxiety.
He feigned a yawn with elbows spread
And fingers dovetailed o'er his head,
Then twirled mustache into a cue,
Then on his sword-hilt thrummed tattoo;
He turned, he glanced, he glowered, he —
                                        Hark!
In Donald comes with Captain Stark.

"Le capitaine?" inquired the Gaul
With smile and courtesy finical.

But Eben knew his part to play,
And posed with grace as recherché;
To meet the courier as a knight
Was both politic and polite;
So Eben to this son of France
Bowed with the courtliest complaisance,
For Eben's manly form and face
Were equalled only by his grace.

The courier, looking haught and grave,
His message now to Eben gave.

Calm Eben's look did not betray
The wrath within.
                    The order read—
(Blotted and dashed and boldly spread):

" *To Captain Stark:*
                    Make no delay—
Quick join the ranks.—With horse and foot
Forward we march on Kawanute.
Haste! Vive le Roi!—Done with his seal.
Halt at your peril!
                    Denonville."

His blood leapt reddening, to resent
Command so curt and insolent;
But, prudent, Eben held in check
A wrath that tinged both face and neck,
And quick he seized his ready quill—
Wielding a pen or sword with skill—
Suppressed his ire within his throat,
And bold, with heavy hand he wrote

Like flourished script of skater's heel,
And fearless:

"*To Mons. Denonville*:
Your threats are but as blustering wind.
I war no more with Kawanute.
We join your ranks when we're too blind
  To see a Frenchman, or to shoot.
Sharp-shooters we—all men of mark—
You'll find us so.
                    Yours,
                        Eben Stark."

He folded, sealed, delivered it,
  With well-feigned haste and vigilance,
  As if the glory and pomp of France
Were all within that message writ!
  And feigning look of anxious care
  For safety of the messenger,
  He bade the Frenchman thus beware:
"Lose not the trail thro' forest wide;
Wild are the woods—the way is dim—
Beset with skulking savage grim."
The courier trembling, terrified,
  At Eben stared, and begged of him
  What Eben gladly gave—a guide.

No host e'er granted the behest
Of titled guest in silk and lace,
With blander smile and courtlier grace
Than Eben granted this request!
Turning to Scot in highland plaid,
In guise of deep concern he said:
"Go, Donald, for his way is dark—
    'T will need your canny vigilance
    To guide the way for 'la belle' France—
Show him the lines,"—said Captain Stark.
And Donald, shrugging, feigned a scowl
As if he heard the forest howl.

XVIII

THE COURIER'S FLIGHT.

With courier forth was Donald sent.
    The one of Gascon never heard;
    The other of Gaelic not a word;
And thro' the forest-wild they went.
Thro' jungles dark and wolfish den
    The sturdy Donald onward led,
    As if from bogles grim he sped
And ghouls from shade Cimmerian.

They strode thro' bushes and mazy brake
As though two lives were now at stake!

The panting courier felt astray.
 He grasped the Scotchman's plaid behind.
"Voila!" he cried; and, pointing, signed
That rearward was his homeward way.
"Whoop!" Donald yelled, and motion made,
 Around his head like scalping-knife,
 As if the woods in rear were rife
With whoop and tomahawk and blade,—
And "Whoop!" came answers wild and fast;
 Their rear was rife with shriek and yell —
 (But Donald knew the voices well!)
The quaking Frenchman paled aghast!
On comes the foe with trampling crash —
Dim forms are seen thro' lightning's flash.

Forward the twain thro' jungles went
 (Like swift Cyllenius thro' the glades
 Hustling the suitors to the shades),
As if from horrors imminent.
Behind, the courier panting-pale
Still clutched the tartan of the Gael!

On, on they sped; thro' dens they fled
  And gruesome haunts with glaring eyes;
  And Donald cringed to half his size,
And glowered as if at bogles dread.
Lightning revealed his ghastly face
Turned on the Frenchman in grimace.

Then on thro' bush and brambly brake,
  In phantom glen and dark ravine
  Startling the wolf and wolverine,
The screeching owl and hissing snake.

"Is it a nightmare grim and ghast?"—
  The courier thought.—"Am I an elf?
  Or is it I . . . am I myself?" . . .
And o'er his face one hand he passed
  While the other held in loving gripe
  His one true friend—the tartan stripe!

. . . Tho' darkling horrors gloomed before
  He dreaded most the foe behind:
  With whoop and screeching limbs, the wind
Now joined the diabolic roar!

The gale it blew, and to and fro
  The forest bowed before the blast;

The cloven pine flew headlong past
And thundering shook the earth below.
  Thus warred the earth and elements
  As thro' the gloom they scurried thence.

But lo! keen Donald's peering sight
  Caught glimpse afar of flaming torch,
(He kenned it was no friendly light!),
  And darted with a sudden lurch
Into the thicket's gloom of night.
  Sundered from courier, forth he sped,
  Leaving behind a tartan shred.

Startled, astounded, and aghast,
  Clutching a shred of highland plaid,
  The courier glowered in dusky glade,
And "hola! ho!" cried wild and fast;
And, reckless, dashed in frenzied fume
  Into the tangled chaparral,
  With outcry shrieking tragical
For guide who vanished in the gloom.

" *Show him the lines :* "
             That torch showed clear
The lines the captain meant were near!

Homeward went Donald light and gay—
  Shorn of the courier's tugging weight,—
  Bounding o'er log and bush elate,
Nor dens nor bogles in his way!
He left the courier groping on
  Thro' tangled mazes dark and dense—
  In forest's vast circumference
Thridding the jungles wild—alone!
"Show him the lines!" was the order sent.
What lines? Not French, 't was evident,—
But Donald knew what Eben meant.

And Donald now to camp again
  Came blithesome as from highland reel,
  And singing loud, *"cha till mi tuille!"*
A Gaelic strain with wild refrain:
"Cha till mi tuille—cha till mi tuille!"
  Sang Donald; and a merry score
  Joined chorus: "we return no more!"
Fitting reply to Denonville.

They gather round in jocund group,
  No wrangling rout of sack and port;
  But sparkling rose the bubbling sport
As Donald gave his mimic "whoop!"

At bogles feigned he glared askance,
  And cringed aghast in grisly awe;
  Then whooped again, and shrieked "hola!"—
Then joined the laugh at "la belle" France.
  A wild strathspey—a highland reel—
  He led the scout of Denonville!

XIX

PEACE!

What though without the blast may howl,
  There 's peace within—the pipes are lit!
  O wand of Peace, of Mirth, of Wit!—
What magic in that little bowl!
  Now Ronald sung ecstatic lay—
  A pæan for the Pipe of Clay;
  The group betimes their lips they wipe,
  And swell the chorus of The Pipe:

1

O Pipe benign! Sweet calm is thine—
Soothing the murmurs of a world.
This bowl in air whirls cark and care,
Cloudward in wreaths of fragrance whirled!

CORO.

With purple, wreathe
This brow of mine—
In fragrance breathe,
O Pipe benign!

2

'Neath azure bays we sing thy praise,
  O Pipe, with Peace cerulean crowned!
The carl and king united sing,
  And rule THIS realm of Blue Profound!

CORO.

With purple, wreathe
  This brow of mine—
In fragrance breathe,
  O Pipe benign!

The storm is past. The winds are low.
  That Peace of Song Benign doth brood
  Above the murmurs of the wood—
Lulling the sough of crooning bough.

XX

EBEN'S PERPLEXITY.

Now in the camp they sink to rest,
  And soon their weary eyelids close;
  Save one . . . in vain he seeks repose,
Perplexed with doubts that harry his breast.
  No spectres grim before him rise,
  But a fancied form in Beauty's guise.

The moonlight glimmering on the tent
  Made fretted meshes through the trees—
  Flitting and flirting with the breeze
In a fantastic tournament;
And Eben watched the shadowy dance:
  "The light and shade are Love and Doubt—
  They shift and shuffle in giddy bout,—
O phantom Love—thou spirit of Chance!"
  Complained he thus in harassed mood,
  Of Love and Love's vicissitude.

"'If stars be bright—if woods be still—
  I will,' she said . . . 'IF!'—if, she will.
O fickle IF!—but half a breath,
Yet 't is of Love the shibboleth!"
So Eben mused. Sagacious he,
But young in Love's philosophy;
  For in the creed of Love 't is shown
· That Doubt and Jealousy are one.

———

By Eben's side wise Ronald lay
  In dreamless sleep oblivious,
  Till sudden, as from incubus,
A thrust awoke him.
            "Ronald! say,

What do you know of pearls and leaves ?"

As miser wakes, beset with thieves,
Startled he 'woke in blank amaze—
Staring with a bewildered gaze.

(Deeming his words not understood,
Eben, with elbow thrust, renewed:)

" Ronald! what means the coronet
    When pearls above the leaves are set ?"

Ronald now deeming Eben's brain
Clouded with dreams and fancies vain,
Answered as one who by degrees
Would break a dreamer's fantasies:

" The answer, Captain, I could tell,
    If question were more tangible;
    If weighty as your elbow thrust
    'T would crush a boulder into dust!"

EBEN.

Come! learnéd Ronald, for you know,
Give answer—jollity forego.

RONALD.

Well—serious: with a mystic guess
I'll answer like the Pythoness:
You wandered in your dreamy trance
Thro' dazzling halls of gay romance;
With pomp and pageant, wit and wine,
Feasted with lords and ladies fine;
In dreams you sate on fancy's throne
Claiming an earldom as your own —
And donned the coronet of earl *
Emblazoned bright with leaf and pearl.

EBEN.

'T was not a trance.

RONALD.

       Perhaps romance?

EBEN.

No lord, no knight —

RONALD.

       Nor ladies bright!
Nor ducal halls with Beauty dight!

---

* An earl's coronet is garnished with pearls above strawberry
leaves; that of a marquis, with pearls between the leaves: that
of a viscount, with pearls only.

EBEN.

No castle, duke, nor coronet—

RONALD.

No moonlit nook—nor soft regret?
No love? oh, no! nor sweet brunette!

EBEN.

Ah! Ronald, *you* have dreamt of her—
Or are you seer and sorcerer?

RONALD.

As bird that flies to heaven's dome
Again returns to th' eyrie Home,
So we that fly o'er hill and glen
To th' eyrie, LOVE, return again. . . .
Like dazzling glance from wing of dove
Is bright Romance to Life and Love!

EBEN.

Ecstatic Ronald! now I know
A barb hath pierced your bosom, too,—
"Who *is* she?"—as of old 't was said
When mischief thro' the kingdom sped.

Fling by restraint, and banish fear,
Whate'er the tale, 't is sacred here.
Did I not thus a trust impart
Though sacred sealed within my heart?
Did I not tell of her who came
And touched my stoic heart with flame?—
Bright ONNALINDA—sweetest name!—
Kind Heaven! keep watch and ward above her,
And waft her dreams of love—

RONALD.

     —and *lover!*

EBEN.

Now, while the camp is deaf and dumb,—
Heedless of song or story,—come!
Ronald, the tale!

RONALD.

    Would that to me
Were given a tale of chivalry!
But since (best friend!) you ask, I 'll give
My life in briefest narrative,
And only here and there select
The mile-stones of the retrospect.

The epochs in our lives are three;
  And here we grope in rifts between
  The IS ... the WAS ... the MIGHT HAVE BEEN.
From gleaming hills of youth we see
The glorious lands of Is to Be.
  In twilight's vale of Is we pause
  To mourn the fading light of WAS.
Then midnight glooms the earth and sky,—
"Alas! it Might Have Been"—we sigh.

You see me gay; you hear me jest,
And join the laugh with sturdy zest.
"*Happy?*" Have you so soon forgot
"The winds may blow that whistle not!"

Captain! I feel that when we stray
From Heaven's path, and grope our way—
When gloom and fear make us repent—
The light of Mirth is to us sent.
The godless caitiff never laughs
Save when the blatant bowl he quaffs.
  . . . But, to my tale:—

XXI

RONALD'S TALE.

         "My story brief:
'T is years since an Algonquin chief
With half his tribe of warriors red,
In war's dread trappings habited,
Rushed on our hamlet. Child was I
Of scarce ten years, and yet the cry—
The war-whoop wild, and wail of grief
Brought by that red Algonquin chief—
Sound in the ear of memory.
Never can I forget the look
My mother gave me when he took
My hand from hers!—that agony
   That blanched her dear sweet face to snow!
Her outstretched arms' beseeching plea,
   Her livid lips,—forget? ah, no.

"On steeds so fleet, away! away
  They hurried us in wild array:
  Over the hills and forest dales
  They hurried us on winding trails.
  . . . Once from a hill I turned my eyes
  And saw the whirling smoke arise —

Loved hamlet! . . . Yet one gleam of hope—
I saw upon the distant slope
One little cottage of the group;
It stood apart—untouched by flame.
I caught my mother's eye; there came
Over her pale dear face a smile,
   As if ''t is ours!' to say to me,
To cheer me, tho' her heart the while
   Was breaking in its agony.
. . . That was the last, last beam of joy
From those sad eyes on me—her boy."

(Here Ronald paused and turned away—
In manly tears he silent lay.
And Eben, brave but tender bred,
Laid gentle palm on Ronald's head.
. . . A sob . . . and Ronald rose, and went,
Followed by Eben, out the tent.
There sat the comrades, eye-bedewed,—
O brave and loving brotherhood!
. . . And Ronald now his tale renewed:)

"Onward we sped o'er hill and dale,
   Through bush and bog and forest trail,

An Indian's arm around me flung,
And to that dusky arm I clung.
My mother hung, like drooping leaf,
On the proud arm of Indian chief.
It was a blest but sad relief
To me, her little boy, to see
He held her gently, tenderly.
—As on we sped thro' wood and glade,
Sudden from out an ambuscade
A hostile tribe upon us burst
With fiendish whoop and yell accurst!
Confusion dread! Quick as a thought
We whirled like leaves in tempest caught.
I only saw—once glancing round—
My mother sinking to the ground.
Straight at the Algonquin chief there sped
A mightier chief, of look renowned,—
My mother sank. The Algonquin fled.
Again my mother a captive led!
Plucked from the ground at his palfrey's feet,
   And held on a mightier arm again,
Swift was she borne on palfrey, fleet
   As the hetman's steed of the wild Ukraine.
O'er the distant hill against the skies
She vanished in mist of my streaming eyes.

But ah! even yet one little ray
 Of childish hope—so slight, but sweet—
That somehow, somewhere, in some way,
 The mother and her boy would meet:
That mighty chief's chivalric grace
Bespoke a hero of his race.

"August of mien, heroic mould,
 Like Argive chief on Ilium's plains;
His lenient eye so gently bold,
His bearing proud and stately, told
 Of gentle blood that coursed his veins.
Methought his look a heart revealed—
Sweet hope! he would the captive shield.

"Onward! and onward still we pressed.
 The gloom of night came darkly down.
Then in a valley to the west
 We struck their camp—an Indian town.
The people—lads and maids—came out
 To greet their little pale-face guest;
They knew not how their merry shout
 Sank doleful in my little breast.
'O mother! mother!'—thus cried I—
What could I do but stand and cry?

"That long dark night I sobbing lay
Calling for her — so far away!
Trembling, I sobbed in low lament,
Lying within the Algonquin's tent.
But one, one solace to my grief,
The little daughter of the chief
Seemed touched with pity, for I knew
When I was crying she cried too!
... Thus the long night dragged slowly by —
O night of wailing misery!
When morning shone —

    (But why prolong
This tale of wretchedness and wrong?)
The days, and oh! the nights, dragged by.
 The weeks — the months — a captive still!
Spring came, but neither sunny sky
 Nor song of bird awoke one thrill.
One morn the chief, in gayer mood,
 Bade them two ponies bring, and he,
 With merry Indian girl and me,
Went riding through the echoing wood.
Thus she and I together rode,
He leading through the solitude.
Afar we ranged on woodland trail
Thro' sunny glade and scented dale.

The chief he laughed well-pleasèd to see
That oft I joined with gayety
The gladsome little maiden's glee!
And on we rode till from a height,
Behold! there loomed upon our sight
A little cottage far away,
Bright-gleaming in the sunny day.
As a fond father joyful greets
 His long-lost wanderer at his door,
Then shrinks appalled — his son he meets
 Whose brain, so bright in days of yore,
 Is wrapt in darkness evermore,—
Thus sudden beamed that cottage bright ...
As sudden wrapt in pall of night,—
The LIGHT of Home — ah! where was she?
O dark and dreary vacancy!

"The little maiden wondered why
So sudden mute and sad was I;
How could she know the tears that fell
Told sadder tale than lips could tell!

"No life, no sound — and all around
A hamlet's ashes strewed the ground.
We entered; and so strange the sound

I turned, and stood without the door—
I durst not tread that silent floor!
... Some dusty books they brought me out
That on the floor were strewn about—
Books that I 'd lay on mother's knee
And read to her, and she to me.

"Again we mounted, and away
　　Homeward we rode—I called it home!—
We reached it as the weary day
　　Sank in the twilight's deepening gloom.
And the long days drew slowly by—
　　The days to seasons; these to years!
And then with rising dignity
　　Came manhood's heart—its hopes and fears.

"(. . . Captain! you smile,—) yes, as I grew
　　She grew—a charming maiden too.
From little dusky Indian bud
Blossomed a sweet rose of the wood—
Morn's dewy rose of womanhood!

"A chieftain's daughter—proud was she
　　To all the tribe, but smiled on me!

" I taught her all our books could teach —
　　Bright pupil she!—she learned so well
She knew the sweetest part of speech
　　And read my heart ere she could spell!

"And as she grew in years and lore
　　I taught her what the sages writ;
She learned all that and something more,
　　Then SHE taught ME what they omit!
And much that never was told in print
Shone from her dark eye's tender glint!

" But now a threatening cloud arose,
　　That, ever-widening, darker grew
　　And 'tween us and the sunny blue
Of happy skies would interpose;
　　Upon us darkly frowned askant
　　The eye of Envy vigilant:

"A warrior, brave and lithe and young,
　　Reserved and sly—his words but brief;
His belt with many a trophy hung
　　Won him the favour of the chief.

"As wise besieger first would seize
    The bastioned heights above the town,
Then turn from these his batteries
    And send his iron summons down;
So he first won the chief, and thus
From haughty heights looked down on us.

"One morn she trembling came to me;
    Her pallid cheeks with tears were wet;
I read our fate!—'t was misery . . .
    Our loves—our lives!—with woes beset.
She sobbing wailed:
                'It cannot be . . .
    O would that we had never met!'

"She told me then, in hurried breath,
    Of midnight plot that warrior planned—
He spoke of snares, but hinted DEATH!—
    Her sire, too, heeding his demand.

"To stay was death. To part was—what!
    For one 't was life—for both 't was woe!
In tears the aid of Heaven we sought—
    Its purpose, ah, could we but know!
But part we must . . .

That day went by.
In evening's gloom again we met
In wonted covert silently,
While agony our souls beset.

"O clinging anguish of that love
That ends for aye in one last kiss!...
In prayer she gazed to Heaven above
And, trembling like a wounded dove,
'Adieu!'—she wailed...then gave me THIS."

(And Ronald from his bosom drew
A little disk that argent shone.
He sat in silence. He alone
Its hidden spring and meaning knew.
A tear to Eben clear revealed
'T was shrine in sacred silence sealed.
—With vulgar quest we will not pry
Into its sacred privacy.
...Then Ronald, rising as he spoke,
With hurried words the silence broke:)

"But, Captain, see! the moon is high,
'T is drawing late ... '*My life since then?*'
I 've seen two hemispheres of men!
I 've seen the blue Italian sky;

I' ve sailed the murky Indian seas,
And roamed the far antipodes;
Auld Scotia have I lingered in —
Rapt with the glories of Kilin!
I 've seen the gay cachuca whirls
Of fairy-footed Zian girls;
And rose-lipt nymph of Gulistan
In slumber feigned on soft divan;
But all, ay, all from memory fade
Save her — that dear Algonquin maid!
Only in silence of the night —
In dreams our meetings we renew,
Then fades her vision from my sight,
   I only hear her last 'Adieu!'
... So, Captain! all is vanity —
   My life 's a shot athwart the dark!—
And, save a sad-sweet memory,
   I 've just one friend ... you — Eben Stark!"

He ceased.
   Into the slumbering tent
Eben and Ronald silent went.
Ronald to sink in slumber deep,
Eben to dream in fitful sleep.

XXII

How fares the messenger of France!
  Bewildered, torn, and sore beset—
  Thridding the maze of jungles yet—
He gropes thro' forest's dark expanse.
No torch that canny Donald kenned
Showed to the Frenchman foe or friend!

And ONNALINDA?—slumbering yet
Tho' portents dark the night beset.
But wake her not tho' omens rise
To threat with gloom love's azure skies;
Startle her not!—that preságe dun
May flee before the morning sun.

O'er misty vale and purple height
Dark are the brooding wings of night.

XXIII

CLOUDS.

"If stars be bright—if woods be still,"
  Repeated Eben as he 'woke.

He gazed abroad. The morning broke
With presage vague across the hill;
   And in the west a menace dark
Of clouds that gloomed the canopy:
"Depart, O gloom! from earth and sky . . .
   We meet to-night!"—said Eben Stark.

Uprose that cloud so dark and dank,
And as it rose his ardour sank.

XXIV

COURAGE!

The day drew on—the sunless day—
   And slowly verged to its decline;
   But low in the west an azure line
'Twixt cloud and earth stretched far away.

And Eben gazed with watchful eye:
   Behold! bright Hope peered thro' the clift;
   And wider grew the azure rift,
And brighter Eben's ecstasy!
   Auspicious promise! still it grew
   A widening rift of gold and blue.

Then sudden sunset bursting forth,
  Blazed all the hill-tops of the West,
  And, glancing, touched each mountain crest,
And smiled across the happy earth,
  Till Twilight came in mystic hue
  And over the earth her mantle threw.

Twilight! and all the woods are still.
  The blinking stars came, one by one.
  Eben thro' woodlands went alone,
As once, with finger-tips a-thrill!

And onward, onward to the tryst!
  Lighter his feet with heart elate.
  The stars are bright—the winds abate—
The skies of Hope are amethyst!

While to the nook he wends his way
  We stand in shadow of the tent,
And list to what his comrades say
  Of him who thro' the darkness went;
For now 't is much their wont to prate
Of Eben's rambles long and late!
We may o'erhear, 'tween song and jest,
From comrades gay who know him best,

Of deed or tale that tells the man
Better than panegyric can.

Listen! his comrades in the camp
　Now jest of walks in forest dark.
They know not LOVE is a brighter lamp
　Than moon or star to Eben Stark!
None know but Ronald Kent, and he
Keeps to himself the mystery.

And thus of Eben they joke and prate —
　One said: "He's timid." One: "He's daft";
And one (a Scot): "He's coy and blate";
　And one: "He's love-sick!"
　　　　　　　And they laughed,
Till Ronald, vexed with jest and joke,
Turned sharply on them, and he spoke:

"Fools! for ye know not what ye say.
　One glance of his in battle-fray
　Will keener pierce by simple threats
　Than all your swords and bayonets!
'*Timid?*' say tender.　Had ye known
　What I have seen, when he alone

(Of all a shrieking multitude)
'Twixt Innocence and Horror stood —
Confronting calm a howling foe —
Varlets! ye had not jested so."

(And Ronald's comrades saw that he
Was vexed with their hilarity.)

"Pardon,"—they said—"but he's away,
And now (th' old saw) 'the kittens play.'
Tell us the tale. We love to hear
The very name we hold so dear.
There's not a man in all our band
But would 'twixt Death and Eben stand!
Tell us the tale."
            And Ronald Kent
Stroked his dark beard and bowed assent
With brow austere, as if he brought
Tidings with solemn import fraught.

We peer thro' opening in the tent —
See! sparkling eyes of merriment
As if on merry mischief bent!—
Some festive quip his comrades plan
As Ronald now his tale began:

"'T was off the coast of—"

    "Ho! hold! hold!"—

On him they broke—

    "That tale's too old.

A hundred ballads all begin,

''T was off the coast,'—they're old as sin!"

And straightway all began to roar

Stale ballads both of sea and shore,

Drawling and quavering "ands" and "ers"

To mimic their great-grandmothers.

A dozen ballads bawled at once,

 And ceasing but as breath would fail!

Then Ronald, frowning, made response:

"Comrades! now hear me for the nonce—

 Your jests are gross. Give me your ears:

 Your quips, perchance, will end in tears.

 I tell no ballad coarse and stale;

 'T is new as true my simple tale."

Their sparkling mirth they ceased anon,

And their eyes grew moist as the tale went on:

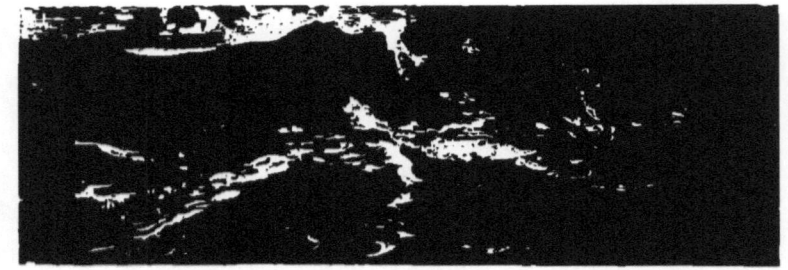

XXV

THE BALLAD OF THE STRANGER.

1

'T was off the coast of Scarboro'
  In sixteen eighty-three;
An April night fell lowering
  Upon an angry sea.
And on the heights above the town
Was many a watcher gazing down,
And murmuring with a shrug and frown:
  "A woful night 't will be!"

2

The wind across the surges
  Came howling to the land;
In foaming wrath the breakers
  Came bounding on the strand;

When with a voice from turret high
Sounded aloud that startled cry:
"A wreck! a wreck!—Shoremen ahoy!
  She's plunging for the land!"

3

Down from the heights went skurrying
  The wreckers to the shore,
And women wild, who seaward smiled
  Hopeful an hour before!
The ship—great God!—in flames her prow!—
The flames are bursting from her bow!
She speeds full sail!—
            Thank Heaven the gale
  Is blowing to the shore!

4

Red are the waves before her—
  Each crest a flaming brand!
With tongues of wrath and fiery breath
  She leaps toward the strand.
"Ahoy! ahoy!"—the trumpet rings—
See! on the hidden reef she springs!
To rock she clings,—
            On rock she swings
  Her larboard to the land.

5

A thousand shrieks of terror
  Arise from ship and shore!
" Launch! launch the boats!"—the trumpet notes
  Blare out above the roar.
But every boat, from beach or deck,
Like shells the breakers crush and wreck.
Stranded she stood ...

                  In fire and flood ...
  But a hundred yards from shore.

6

Down to the beach a stranger
  Stept calmly thro' the crowd;
He doffed his cloak, and up he spoke
  With startling voice and loud:
" Come on with me, the bravest three! . . ."
  (In yawl they plunged into the sea.)
" Give me the rope!—

                  Cowards are we,
  To cringe at such a shroud?"

7

Athwart the breakers plunging
  Went gallant men and yawl;
A rope they bore, the coil on shore
  Trailed out with snaky crawl.

Behold! they sink!—

        A mountain wave
Buries them deep in yawning grave!
A shriek! a wail from women pale
    The bravest souls appall.

8

Up! see!—the dauntless heroes
    Upon the surges rise!
"Praise God!" a shout from ship and shore
    Breaks upward to the skies.
"Courage!"—peals out that stranger's shout—
He strikes the wreck . . .

        He leaps on deck . . .
His rope ties fast to mizzen mast,
    And, *"Down the rope!"* he cries.

9

Swift, one by one, like pigeons
    From startled cote, they pour—
They glide on rope through breakers
    Hand over hand to shore . . .
The flames! the flames!

        With hiss and gnash
Sternward their tongues of fire they flash,
And on the flames the surges dash
    With seething shriek and roar!

10

The last man 's o'er the taffrail —
   Alone the stranger . . . No!
Horrors!—up from the hatchway
   A woman from below!—
Clasping her child, in terror wild
Shrieking:
        "O God! my child! my child!"
To the stranger's breast her babe she prest
   In agony of woe.

11

Tho' singed with fire that hero
   To his breast the babe he bound:
Then to the sea leapt mother and he—
   She clasping him around.
Now on the rope, hand over hand,
   Thro' breakers plunging for the strand—
"Hold to the rope! it *burns!*"—
        From land
Rings out the trumpet-sound.

12

A shuddering cry uprises
   From thousands on the lee —
The rope it parts, and flaming darts
   And hisses in the sea!

" Hold to the rope!"

                    Alas! a wave
O'erwhelms him deep — that hero brave!
Down, down, they sink into that grave —
    The mother, babe, and he.

13

There is a sudden silence
    Hushes the land in awe,
As over the sands a hundred hands
    That willing rope they draw. . . .
" PRAISE GOD, THE LORD!"
                    Bursts sudden cry
From thousand voices raised on high. . . .
See! on the land, above the strand,
    Silent and pale they lie!

14

In fixéd grasp that hero
    The rope still firmly holds!
And firm his teeth with clench of death
    That mother's sleeve enfolds!
Oh, fearful sight! — more rueful seem
Those faces in the lurid gleam. . . .
But — hark! he speaks!
                    He stirs! he wakes!
He starts as from a dream!

15

And the mother's lips are quivering
  As if to speak . . . and hark!
She calls her child . . . she gazes wild
  Toward the burning barque.
The stranger smiled; unbound his breast . . .
The babe lay smiling in its nest!
The mother shrieked in rapture wild:
"My child! my child!—
              Thank God! my child!"

16

The multitude came surging,
  And round that stranger prest,—
With prayer and cry that reached the sky
  That hero brave they blest.
But not a word the stranger spoke . . .
He calmly smiled,—
          He donned his cloak,
And, bowing, vanished in the dark.
"*Who was the hero?*" . . . EBEN STARK!

And Ronald ceased. The camp was still.
His comrades mute a moment stood,
Their eyelids quivering and bedewed
With tenderness they would conceal,—
A moment mute:—uprose a shout
That 'woke the woodlands round about
And echoed in the forests dark:
"God bless the hero—Captain Stark!"

'Tis such a deed reveals the man
More than all panegyric can.
Let simple story-song like this
Be Eben's apotheosis.

XXVI

THE SEARCH.

The night drew on. The moon arose
As Eben neared the nook. No sound
Broke on the night—a calm profound:
Too calm—too still, the deep repose!
One lone cicada, grieving, made
A lonelier silence in the glade.

"She comes not . . . Did she smile on me!"
(He muttered in soliloquy,)

"Ah! now methinks that 'neath her smile
Lurked hidden witchery and wile!
Was sorcery, the serpent, hid
Beneath her soft eye's fringéd lid?
No, no! that face so sweet! so fair!
There could be no illusion there.
And yet . . . No, no!—be still, O heart!
No guile was there—no sorcerer's art.
What did she say . . . 'if' so and so—
  And, 'if there wake no jealous eye' . .
  Ah! that 's the wherefore and the why!—
She loves him . . . That mute warrior?. . . No!
And yet . . . O cursed doubt!—I go."
He rose. Distrustful and distraught
His homeward path he, frowning, sought.
"Fled! Fled, my Starlight!—Cold and dark
Are heaven and earth!" said Eben Stark.
Halting, he mused . . . then on his track
He turned, and slowly wandered back.
He listened . . . and, with sudden thought,
HER pathway to the nook he sought.
His way along the river led—
  Her pathway at last eve's adieu—
"O peaceful river!" sad he said—
  "Would that my path were peaceful too!"

Then at a thicket's marge he stayed
  And, peering stilly through, he met
A sudden gleam of moonlit glade—
  Bright knoll, like gem in dew-drops set.
And lo! a form was kneeling there
In saintly attitude of prayer,
Her palms together devoutly prest
Were raised in supplication blest;
Her pale sweet face to Heaven above
·Seraphic beamed with heavenly love.
There—there her sainted mother slept,
And there sad Onnalinda wept.
Upon her cheek in moonlight clear
Glistened a lonely trembling tear;
While that beloved name to bless,
Her sweet lips breathed in tenderness:

  " Mother, O mother! on thy breast
    Thy wearied child again would rest—
    Thy loving arms around me prest.

  Mother, O mother! dark my way
    When from thy grave I lonely stray;
    In tears I kneel by thee and pray.

  Mother, O mother! join to-night
    Thy prayer with mine for Heavenly light—
    Oh, dark, so dark! my path to-night."

Above the grave each dewy blade
  Low with a tear of pity bent;
No purer they than she who prayed
  Kneeling with them in low lament.
Then she arose, and from the glade
  Along her pathway slowly went.
Erewhile had Eben thence withdrawn —
Too sad that face to gaze upon:
He 'd not profane with curious eye
That hallowed scene of sanctity.

XXVII

IN THE NOOK.

Within the nook once more they met;
  As one would meet a lovely saint
  Whose very smile held a restraint,
He met the woodland anchoret.
A touch of palms . . . Magnetic thrill!
  It tingling reached his finger tips
  And drew her hand up to his lips,
And drew her nearer, closelier still.
  With look demure and modest grace
  She drew her hand, retired a pace
  And furtive viewed his moonlit face.

Then Eben sat. Apart she stood.
  Her white arm round a moonlit tree
  Glistened with jewelled brilliancy.
A vision of beatitude,
  Revealed in beauteous symmetry
'Twixt Eben and the moon she stood.
And was it thus by maiden's art
  The moonlight fell upon his face
While 'gainst that light she stood apart,
  Outlined, a rounded form of grace?

No more about the bush he beat—
  No more of questions vague and dim—
  He knew as vague she'd answer him,
Bright Onnalinda—shrewd as sweet!—
  That silent brave—that sphinx obscure—
  In silence Eben must endure.

Thwarted, he knew his quest were vain;
  And eager now that she renew
  The tale that ceased when whistle blew,
He turned to happier themes again—
  Asking of home beyond the sea,
  Of kindred and of ancestry.

With searching eye she long had scanned
  Each feature of his noble face;
  And pleased, she found not even a trace
Of artifice in treason planned.
  That face of calm sincerity
  Was pledge secure.

                    " You seem " (she said,)
" Like knight of whom my mother read
  In famous tales of chivalry,
  Whose sword knew neither wrong nor rust:
  In such a knight shall woman trust."

With timid grace she closer drew
  Her gown around her ankles trim,
And featly through the silvery dew
  Near Eben came and sat by him.

She held, and tenderly caressed,
  A wild rose glistening with the dew
  Of moonlit mound whereon it grew;
And oft to it her lips she pressed
  While sweetly, softly tremulous,
  She told her tale to Eben thus:

XXVIII

HER DISCLOSURE.

"You ask of me," she coyly said,
  "My life's strange story—to renew
  The tale that ceased when signal blew,—
(Pleased do we go where kindly led!)
—You marvel why in this abode
Of glen and glade and pathless wood
I seek retreat in solitude.
Know, then, that in my pulses beat
Two mingled currents wild and fleet,—
Tingeing my veins like ruby wine
Leaps the proud blood of ancient line
Whose swarthy knights and forest kings
No records reach, no poet sings.

"You wondered when last night I said
  The mother of the woodland girl
Was nobly born and nobly bred—
  The daughter of a Scottish earl!
A lordly castle broad and high
Was home of her nativity.

A castle girt by cliff and scaur,
O'erlooking lovely vale afar,
And in that vale's expanse of green
A lake that shone in azure sheen
Lovelier than this Genesee
Hemm'd with its verdant livery;
An emerald marge its bosom bound,
　With pink and silver shells bedight,
Like dazzling necklace clasped around
　Beauty's soft neck of snowy white.
Northward the purple mountains high
　Arose thro' veil of silver mist,
　And in the haze clandestine kiss'd
Each flirting cloud that hovered by.

"My mother told of paths that wound
　The heathery mountain sides around;
Of hedgerows sweet that lined her way
Thro' blooming lanes of daisied May,
A lowly cottage here and there—
The home of hardy highlander
Who, when the toilsome day was o'er,
　And grateful shades of evening fell,
With dame and bairns about the door
　Would merrily make the pibroch swell;

From crag to crag the peal resounding,
   Echoing thro' each bosky glen,
Till, from the distant cliffs rebounding,
   Ebbing in murmurs back again.
And thus each eve, as twilight fell,
She heard the sound of pibroch swell,
And down the Dochart's winding stream
Echo, and die into a dream.

"And oft my mother fain would tell
   Of lordly home and stately hall,
   Of marbled floor and pictured wall,
And statues standing sentinel;
Of arms and armour, blazoned shield
Dinted in many a stubborn field,
Battered cuirass and splintered lance
(Grotesque and grim inheritance!)
That told of valiant knight's romance.
Of such my mother oft would tell—
Of sounds and scenes she loved so well.
. . . But over that home a shadow fell:

"One morn came love. A youth he came,
   Of manly port and fair to see.
Unknown to fame; tho' fair his name
   He boasted not of ancestry.

My mother, then a winsome girl,
　In wisdom well as beauty grew:
She deemed (tho' daughter of an earl)
　The smile of worth the guerdon true.
Not so her sire. His coronet
　He valued more than brain or heart—
A penny more than violet,
　His coat of arms the end of art:

> With gules upon an argent field;
> An azure fesse athwart the shield;
> A chevron or, enraftered, fret
> With purple-tinctured barrulet;
> On dexter chief a blazoned spur,
> An ermine tuft on sinister.

" Such was his coat of arms, and he
　Adored the gairish vanity.

" One eve a groom, officious, told
　Of what his lurking eye espied:
' She walks clandestine in the wold—
　A simple yeoman by her side.'

" Up to his brows in reddening ire
　Arose the feudal blood of sire.

His daughter called . . . 'And can it be—
A wolf among the bleating flocks!
Do pheasants covey with the fox?'
—With taunting trope demanded he.
A gleam from out his darkling eye
Presaged the storm now drawing nigh.
But love—true love, when storms assail,
Is like the birdling in the gale:
It closer, warmer, folds its wings,
And to the limb it firmer clings.

"Ah! could I tell in her sweet way
   My mother's plaint o'er vanished years,
   Upon your cheek would tremble tears
Like dew-drops on the quivering spray;
   But brief I'll tell . . . (As one would look
   But for italics in a book:)

"That yeoman wooed . . .
           He won . . .
                  They wed . . .
Her sire she sought . . .
           He scoff'd . . .
                  They fled . . .
Name, rank, and largess, forfeited.

"Unpitying sire! Nor tear, nor prayer,
  Could touch one tender feeling there.
  Her tears he spurned,—
                  He deemed her dead!...
  To Love she turned—
                  And sought their bread!
  Into the wide, wide world they went.
    They spoke of new worlds in the west—
  True love in deserts is content—
    And thither they would turn their quest.

"One morn, before the ship would sail,
    My mother longed to see once more
    That home, still fondly loved, before
  She bade it evermore farewell.
  That morn of June, by hedgerows sweet
    She went. There, at the postern gate
  Sat her old nurse. In tears they met—
    The poor old nurse, disconsolate,
  Clasped her in arms with kisses, tears—
  The welling fount of happier years;
  For, from a nursling sweet, she grew
  The pet of nurse and household too.
  Along the garden-walk they went;
  The rose and orchis redolent;

But changed, alas! each flower and scent;
And even the bees now seemed to drone
A dolorous moan in monotone. . . .
Ah! home beloved! so dear, so fair,
And she in tears—the rightful heir
A stranger and intruder there!
—The threshold crossed. . .

        Ev'n creak of door
Thrilled her with wonted sounds of yore!
A moment pale she stood, and gazed.
That scene beloved her vision dazed.
Her home no more!—That stately hall
Of marbled floor and pictured wall—
That stairway broad and winding high—
Symbol of grace and majesty!
With strange and vacant look she smiled—
Thinking of cot in western wild:
Her sofa a bench; her chair a chest;
Her home a hovel in the west,
But Love the ever-abiding guest!
O gilded home—without a heart—
With all the painter's, sculptor's art!
Here, niche-enshrined, a saintly statue
Gazes intently up or at you;
There satyrs grim and wild bacchant
Ogle a sphinx or griffin gaunt;

Here Aphrodite smiles at Pan
But weds the grisly Artisan;
There naiads mourn o'er funeral pile
And lo! they see Narcissus smile;
Cassandra here in wailings low,
Foretells great Agamemnon's woe.
'Oh! what are these? A mimic show!'
—'T was thus in scorn my mother cried,
Saying, as up the stair she hied:

"'Oh! what are these, with love unblest?—
Give me the hovel in the west!'

"Above the porch one little room
Sweet with the scent of heather-bloom;
'T was hers—in happier days bestowed:
Books, music, pictures,—loved abode!
She entered.
                Kneeling by her chair,
Her grief broke forth in tears and prayer.

"With streaming eyes and aching heart
    Whose sorrows only tears can tell,
The hour has come—the hour to part
    In anguish of a last farewell!

Then she arose. Such books as hold
　　The gems of thought, of lay and lore,
　　She culled from shelves antique that bore
The wealth of song—the bards of old.

" She used to say:
　　　　　'One book, though small,
Of the great songs 't will hold them all,—
One little page will hold in it
All the grand thoughts each scribe hath writ!'

"—These pearls of prose and poet's lay
She gave the nurse to bear away;
Then wept . . . departing from that door,
To cross its threshold nevermore!

" Down the lone stairway—silent all—
　　She glided, trembling like a bird.
　　She paused. . . .
　　　　　Was it a voice she heard!
She turned across the silent hall
　　And softly entered where he sate,
　　The lonely lord of the estate.
Ah! little did he think that she
　　Would soon be as a buried one
To him for evermore, and he
　　In silence tread his halls alone!

"Through sobs my mother could not speak;
She silent bent, and kissed his cheek;
Then turned away . . .
                        To him as dead . . .
'Farewell—belovéd home!'—she said.
Then to the gate she slow withdrew
Where waited he—the yeoman true.

"The dear old nurse—whose loving care
Ended in grief—stood waiting there,
Lamenting, moaning in despair.
Like mother of him who waits his doom
And sees the fearful moment come,
Around her child her arms she flings—
She sobs and kisses, cries and clings,
Till sinking ere the parting knell,
Nor speaks nor hears a last farewell!
So sank th' old nurse. . . .
                        A last adieu
My mother kissed her, and withdrew.
Behind her, like the fiat of Fate,
Closed with a clang the postern gate!

"—Forth to the world they hie away.
The ship awaits in Firth of Tay.

"... The sails are set. ... Afar they glide
Across the bar to the ocean wide.
Back to the shore they lingering gaze
Till the hills are lost in purple haze.
Home, friends, wealth, rank, all—all resigned;
All? Nay—they leave not all behind—
By Love and Hope their steps are led ...
With Love and Hope they seek their bread!

"... Of weary months 't were vain to tell—
But briefly told (to skip the ground
Like leaf in storm, with skip and bound):
... They came—in a new world to dwell.
Long months went by—and then a year.
A little boy brought sunny cheer;
But woes came fast to chill her joy—
Widowed was she; with orphan boy.
I linger not to tell of tears
    Above her love-devoted dead—
Of toilsome days, of hopeless years:
    A struggle now for life and bread.
... Ah! could she send heart-broken plea
To heedless sire beyond the sea
Lolling in lap of luxury!

" One morn in May came warriors red
　　And tribal chieftain of renown;
　Sudden they came with war-whoop dread . . .
　A prisoner she!—and forth they fled
　　With captive to their Indian town.

" Torn from her child, a mother's grief
　Touched to the heart the noble chief.
　'T is more than woman's wail of woe
　When a mother's tears of anguish flow;
　Her pale sweet face in deep distress,
　He viewed with sacred tenderness.
　Then rose esteem from sympathy—
　Then honoured—then beloved was she,
　At last adored in sanctity."

　　[Think not ye dwellers at your ease
　　On pink divans and tapestries—
　　Think not that love with nomad true
　　Is slow of growth as 't is with you:
　　On flying steed they pluck the rose,
　　　Nor stop to count its petals sweet,—
　　　The flower they pass, on palfrey fleet,
　　For them no longer blows.

Then scorn not, gentles! nor reprove
　These dusky warriors who woo
　With ceremonies brief and few—
Who flying live, and flying love!
Is love less sweet, or sweeter thus,
Because unceremonious?
If sweeter in civilities,
　In court'sies and conventionals,
Then don your wigs, your lutes then seize,
　And sing your loves in madrigals!
... But break no more the thread—O Muse!—
Of her strange story.

　　　　　　　　She renews:]

"Amidst the tribe my mother sate,
Revered as saint immaculate.
　This chieftain of the dusky race
She first esteemed and then admired;
　His tender heart, his noble face,
　His manly form and knightly grace,
Her faith and then her love inspired.
　... Sprung from a royal line was he—
The forest's prime nobility
Whose origin no annals tell,—

A famous chieftain, brave as true:
Was he not worthy, then, to woo
The captive whom he loved so well?
Is merit a mark — a badge of race?
Is honour a tint — a tinge of face?
Nay: Red and White are kith and kin —
Bleached is the Saxon's faded skin.

"Vanished but not — ah! not forgot
Her hours of woe, her years of strife;
Then blame her not — O blame her not
When she became the chieftain's wife!
. . . The seasons came and fled apace.
Beloved, adored by chief was she.
A bright content shone in her face
Save when a cloud from Memory
Passed over, leaving there a trace
Of days, tear-dimmed, that used to be:
Her boy — her boy! Oh! where is he?
Oft in her prayer a tear revealed
A sorrow deep in silence sealed.
Then wintry nights came bleak and long, —
Ah! for the long-lost books of song!
One quiet eve she lonely sighed
For those companions true and tried:

Those pearls of prose and poet's lay
Were over the forests, far away,
Unread, untouched by friend or foe,
Beside the far Ontario.
To know her wish, was, to the chief,
A joy—a spur to action brief:
The swiftest runners sped away
    To Cadaracqui's southern shore;
They flew by night, they flew by day,
    And found those gems of lay and lore;
Then swift o'er vale and wooded height,
Eager to bring the new delight,
They flew by day, they flew by night,
    And back her dainty treasures bore.

"Joy in her home! Sweet Peace and rest . . .
    Swifter the moments fled . . . One morn
    A little woodland girl was born:
Love smiled, and all the years were blest.

"My story's ended . . . It would tire
    To tell of years that glided by.
That chief was Kawanute, my sire,
    That little woodland girl was I."

XXIX

Silent sat Eben in surprise.
　　Her tale, with tenderness replete,
　　Was fraught with charm of lips so sweet,
His wonder glistened in his eyes;
　　And closelier still to him he drew
　　That form that more enchanting grew.

He drew her hand with gentle grace
　　In tender pressure of his own,—
　　She gazing upward to the moon,
And he upon her calm sweet face . . .
　　What need of words his love to tell
　　When silence speaks so well—so well!

　　　A valiant knight of high estate
　　　　Who holds a princess' hand in fee,
　　　Before that queen immaculate
　　　　Shall he not bend a suppliant knee?
　　　While favouring clouds the moon eclipse
　　　Is there a touching at the lips?

　　　Can saintliest "nun, devout and pure,"
　　　　All tenderness of love resist—
　　　Or turn away, with look demure,
　　　　The sweetest lips that ever were kiss'd?
　　　The favouring clouds the moon eclipse—
　　　There is a touching at the lips.

XXX

Leave them. 'T is sacrilege profane
  To scan that scene with vulgar eye;
  Tho' gladly would we linger nigh
And hear that gallant soldier-swain
  Rehearsing tales of errantry—
  Heroic deeds on land and sea,
Of war, of siege and red redoubt,
Of deadly breach and storming shout,
  And of chivalric deeds that stir
  The heart of lovely listener.

He drew her sighs, like him of yore
  With hair-breadth 'scapes and struggles vast;
Ah! were he loved like swarthy Moor—
  "Loved for the dangers he had passed!"

XXXI

DECEIVED?

Is it deceit? And has she planned
  With Beauty's lure some artifice?
  (A wily strategist may kiss
With a stiletto in her hand!)

Beware! beware, brave Eben Stark —
A kiss may lure for a purpose dark.

Last night you said to Ronald Kent:
  "Deceit is never a sin in war!"
Perchance sнe holds this sentiment,
  And comes, with Love, th' ambassador.
What if the sweet of lips you kissed
Were honey of the diplomatist!

Beware! 't was but one eve ago
  We heard her murmuring words like these:
"Well, what if I foil our enemies
With weapon keener than blade or bow!"
  Whether true, or false, she's winning her way,
  For 't was last night we o'erheard her say:
"To-night when the moon shines full in his face
  I'll there read clear each thought in his heart;
  He shall not know, as I stand apart,
How keen my glance each line shall trace."

And shall we blame if she conspire
To thwart the foes of her noble sire? —

One moon ago, so fair to see
  His realm beloved — ancestral home —
  Couched in a vale of peace and bloom,
And slumbering in prosperity,
  With gladdening fields of waving corn,
  And hamlets glittering in the morn ; —
Behold at eve the advancing Gaul !
  Billows of smoke roll over the vale,
  Leaving but ashes and woe and wail —
A Kamsin of fire o'erwhelming all !
  O'er home of that sire red ruin swept,
  And he knelt on the blackened earth, and wept.
So, if she be true, or a luring cheat —
  Bright Onnalinda who would blame
  If she kindle in Eben's heart a flame
To light the way to the Gauls' defeat ?
And what tho' her love — *if* begun in deceit —
Should end in a snare for her own pretty feet !

Tender is Eben, but shrewd and bold
  And ready in war to bear the brunt ;
  But what if he meet and must confront
His own wise maxim and be cajoled :
  " Deceit is never a sin in war "—
  And himself be hoist with his own *pétard.*

If Onnalinda can deceive,
What saint on earth can he believe?
But Eben the MAN would take good care
Of Eben the LOVER, here or there;
If she prove kind as she began
He 'll sink the Soldier in the *Man.*
If she prove false, with purpose dark,
Eben will rise to *Captain* Stark.
If true she is, and so remain,
Lover is he, and tender swain!

XXXII

MISTRUST.

The hour sped on. The twain they part.
　Campward went Eben thro' the wood.
Blither his step, though in his heart
　Still nestled a strange inquietude.

As miner dreams of nugget bright
　But slightly hidden beneath the mould,
And trembling lest the morning light
Reveal to earlier, happier wight
　The marvellous nugget of glittering gold,

So Eben's heart in anxious mood
Stirs with a keen solicitude
Lest other hands his guerdon seize—
Worth all a kingdom's treasuries!
And as he campward went he sighed:
 "Ah! is there aught 'neath heaven secure?
From peering eyes can forests hide
   That star—my life's bright cynosure!"

MISTRUST! an ever-tattling brook
   That winds thro' all Love's heritage! . . .
The head-lines in a lover's book,
   Creeping along from page to page!

So Eben thought, and homeward went,
With just a twinge of discontent
Spurred by a vague presentiment.

. . . And homeward Onnalinda strayed
   Hesitant, thro' the glinting dew;
   A vermeil tinge of deeper hue
Upon her cheek her thoughts betrayed.
   And when she sank in sleep that bloom
   Crimsoned in dreams . . . of whom—of whom?

The muse a moment drops the pen.
 Asleep the world. With presage dark
Night broods above the hill and glen,—
 Beware! beware, brave Eben Stark!
 ... With finger 'twixt the leaves to mark
Midway, we pause to ask again:
 On Onnalinda's cheek the bloom
 Crimsoned in dreams of whom—of WHOM?

ONNALINDA

Part II

"* * * * Your patience this allowing,
I turn my glass, and give my scene such growing
As you had slept between. * * * *
* * * * * What of her ensues
I list not prophesy."

WINTER's TALE, Act iv.

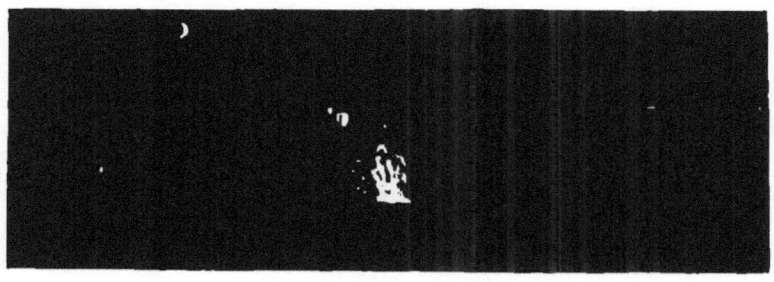

ONNALINDA.

—

I

ALARUM.

THE midnight lowered o'er forest dim.
Forth came the chieftain Kawanute
With blade and bow; on stealthy foot
A score of warriors following him—
Athletes unmatched in bold emprise,
With thews heroic, and eagle eyes:
Peers of the chief—a chosen band—
Alert of ear, and ready of hand.

From crag to crag — from tree to tree —
  Weird shadows flitted thro' the night
  And by the camp-fire's flickering light
Revealed impending jeopardy.

The wavering moan of night-winds gave
  To dying fagot a fitful gleam
  That lanced and tinged with ruddy beam
The Genesee's pulsating wave.

The beams of swift-ascending moon
Silvered the dewy hills of June.

II

But Onnalinda calmly slept,
  Tho' murk and menace lurk and lower;
  Above her peaceful sylvan bower
A sleepless Power a vigil kept.

In dreams she saw a Saxon face,
  Blue-eyed and bearded, bending near ...
  Was Oonak dark, to him a peer —
OONAK, a brave of other race?

In dreams the form of Eben Stark
Arose 'twixt her and warrior dark.

Her name she heard in other tongue —
  In softer, gentler accents fall;
  Ne'er heard so sweetly musical
As when in dreams she heard it sung.

And still she saw, in fancy, near,
  That Saxon face! . . . and nearer still!
  It bends . . . It touches . . .
               Electric thrill! —
Quick-flushed, she wakes! As startled deer
That in the drowse of sultry rain
  Starts at the sudden rifle's ring,
  Dazed in the shock bewildering,
With shivering nerve and misty brain —
So Onnalinda, startled, 'woke
  As if by sudden rifle-shot.
  She 'woke to hear, ah not — ah not
That voice in dreams that tender spoke! —
But on her vigilant ear there broke
  Signals foreboding threat and plot.

The crackling bush, and rustling glade,
  And hurrying tread of stealthy foot,
  Amidst the camp of Kawanute
A quick and wild alarum made.

From limb to limb flew startled owl,
Gazing below with staring scowl.

From rock to rock, from tree to tree —
    Like phantoms in that lurid light —
    Went flitting forms in glimmering flight,
Grim portents of emergency.

Stirred with a quick, prophetic thought,
    Her woman-heart foreboding beat;
    And, gliding forth on agile feet . . .
One glance . . . and all the scene she caught:
    Faces red-tinged in war's array —
    Dread proof of the impending fray!

Her sire she clasped ere rang the whoop —
    Precursor dread of wail and blood! —
    And at her voice he calmly stood,
And around him war's red council group.

" Shame ! shame upon you ! " —

                        Cried the maid —
" Are ye like bats that haunt the night ? —
    And thievish wolves that fear the light ?
Make ye a midnight ambuscade ? "

Flashed her black eyes with fire of scorn;
And warriors quailed with look forlorn.

When Kawanute, the sachem gray,
   Heard Onnalinda's reprimand,
   He instant bade the swarthy band
Defer their dark intent till day.
      (A woman's voice!— It calms the chief
      As evening stills the rustling leaf.)

III

HER FLIGHT.

Soon round the smouldering council-fire
   Lay swarthy forms in slumber deep;
   And soon, while they in heedless sleep
Waited the gleam of morning dire,
   Forth like a barb from Scythian bow,
Or skipping leaf in hurrying storm,
Sped Onnalinda's lissom form
   To seize her oar in swift canoe:

Skilled with the oar her skiff to guide,
To launch, to dart, to veer, to glide.

As rift of lightning thro' the murk
　She pierced the waves athwart the night,
　And swift as shimmering swallow-flight
She skimmed beneath each pendent birk,
With flowing hair flung to the breeze —
　With parted lips and glowing eye . . .
　A form inspired !
　　　　　　　　'T would draw a sigh
From Raphael or Praxiteles :

　Each movement fleet tho' seeming slow;
　Such grace — tho' quick, it seemed not so!

O'er shingly bar, thro' bay and reach,
　Darting, she skimmed the Genesee
　Till, veered in bend beneath the lee,
Her proud canoe rose to the beach —
　Proudly as though it knew it bore
　Queen of the woodland to her shore!

Then up the bank and o'er the brae,
　Featly she tript as chamois light.
　And lo ! she saw, thro' void of night,
A blazing fagot, far away,
　Gleaming upon her gladdened sight.

Fleetly she went, as one would take
Reprieve to martyr at the stake.

Behold! — a tent in yonder glade, —
And there her flight she sudden stayed.

. . . "Fly! fly, O Eben Stark! — red, red
Shall gleam the morning dew!" — she said.

Standing before that wakened tent,
Herald she seemed from heaven sent.

(Did she thus warn her father's foe —
A traitor? Let the sequel show.)

Miraculous apparition she! —
  With eyes aglow and lips apart;
  Another than bold Eben's heart
Would tremble in timidity;
  But well that voice and form he knew,
  And her warm hand in his he drew.
"Dear one!" — said Eben — "here am I
  With twenty marksmen lying near, —
  Brave Onnalinda! do not fear —
These pale-face warriors never fly;

No craven fear o'er trembling stirred
Their rifles, aimed by eyes of blue;
Here 's Ronald Kent with rifle true
    Can trim the wing of humming-bird!"

Sudden she flushed.
                    He spoke one name
That mantled o'er her cheek with flame.
Tho' Eben saw, he knew not why
Quick flushed her cheek, and glowed her eye.

... "Fear not!"—he said—for me or mine—
Nor fear, sweet one, for thee or thine."

She only answered, brief and low:
"Beware at morn of stealthy tread!"
    Then drew her hand from his, and said:
"Beware! ... My task is done. I go."

"Heaven be thy guide, beloved!"
                        He said,
And to his lips her hand he pressed.
    Then with a heart in strange unrest
She turned, and thro' the darkness fled.

The forest's gloom was naught to her —
Auspicious Hope her harbinger!
Onward, intent of thought she sped,
Weighing each word that Eben said.

One name he spoke that seemed to rise
Dim, like a star in dusky skies,
  From out the mists of memory:
A dear but half-forgotten word
That long ago she often heard
  From lips that breathed it tenderly.
And though on other thoughts intent,
She murmured "RONALD" as she went.

Oft gazed she rearward to the tent,—
  Well-pleased she saw a fagot swing—
  A wheel of fire—a flaming ring,
Token of love undying, meant!
  'T was Eben swung that fagot red—
  A flaming halo round his head.

A moment lingering on the brae—
  To view once more the whirling brand,
  Then down the bank, and to the strand,
And in canoe she sped away;

Swift as the shimmering swallow-flight
 She skimmed beneath each pendent birk,
 And as the lightning thro' the murk
She pierced the waves athwart the night.

O'er shingly bar, thro' reach of bay,
 She rounded swift the bending shore
 To mooring, whence, an hour before
With eager oar she dashed away.
 Upon the beach, like bounding doe,
 Again arose her proud canoe.

Stilly she gained her cedar bower
 Above the river's shelving bank;
 And soft on couch of green she sank,
To feign a sleep through all that hour!
 None of that slumbering band of war
 Dreamt of a sweet conspirator!

'Twixt murmurings of the fitful breeze
 She heard the dreaming warriors moan;
 They recked not of events unknown —
Of plots, intrigues, catastrophes:
 So nigh to peril we repose;
 A lurking thorn lies 'neath the rose!

IV

STRATAGEM.

Astir is Eben's camp! . . . And hark
  The hurrying footsteps! Ere the light
  Has touched the sable robe of night,
Swift with his band came Eben Stark
  Thro' forests dim, over hill and dale,
  And up the river's winding trail;
Over crag and scaur and brambly fen
  Wary they came, with rifles keen,
  Till, sudden from cliff o'er dark ravine,
They gaze below:— In shadowy glen
  Lo! prone there lay round flickering fire
  The muffled forms of dusky men—
A score of braves and sachem-sire.

Then stealthy down the craggy steep
  To jutting rock and bush they cling—
  Noiseless as panthers ere they spring—
Warily . . .
      Stealthily . . .
           Hushed, they creep
Till in the glen. There, in array
They wait the first pale gleam of day.

They learn from crafty fox, who takes
The pheasant just as morning breaks.*

V

Now faintly pales the eastern sky
  When lo! from bower above ravine
  Descending, covertly, unseen,
Glides Onnalinda warily;
  The craggy steep dim-lit with glow
  Of lurid camp-fire from below,
  That tinges with a sanguine light
  Each jutting rock and shelvy height.
  In stunted copse of sloe or pine
  Clinging to bush or pendent vine
  She pauses oft — with fervid glance
  Scanning the scene with vigilance.

Then noiseless down the cliff she glides,
And 'neath o'erhanging crag she hides —
Unknown, unseen by hostile bands,
In peering attitude she stands.

* " The sagacious commander will surprise the enemy by falling upon their camps just before daybreak."
                        JOMINI, Art of War, Chap. xxxiv.

VI

Morn breaks! . . .

   The first pale gleam of light
 Brings to his feet the sagamore
And scowling band, of braves a score,—
Behold! —
   In bow-shot on the right
Blank-ranged and bristling in their sight
Are levelled rifles aiming keen
 At every heart of that red band!

 Sudden as thought, with upraised hand
That maiden rises upon the scene,
Upgazing as if to her were sent
A message from the firmament!

Like herald of heaven, august she stands
 With palms outspread 'gainst friends and foes,
 One palm to these, one palm to those —
A barrier 'twixt the hostile bands.

Red warriors marvel at the scene,
(That heavenly maid, those rifles keen,)
They quail. They bend in suppliant mien.

The bravest may the wisest be,
And bow to fate's supremacy.

VII

Bright Onnalinda! forth she tript
　All radiant in her loveliness,
　Smiling, and with adroit address
From bended bows the strings she slipt!
　And e'en her sire now smiling gazed
　As up were levelled rifles raised!

She took the sachem's pipe of peace,
　And lighted it with flaming brand.
　. . . Then Eben Stark and his brave band
Came forth like demi-gods of Greece!
　And all that dusky group, amazed,
　At Eben and Onnalinda gazed.

VIII

Featly as fawn with timid foot
　The maiden stept to Eben brave;
　Her hand to him she smiling gave,
And led him near to Kawanute.

With filial love, so meek, so calm,
  Upgazed she in her father's face;
  And with a dove-like, gentle grace,
In his she laid her lover's palm!
O queenly woman! A sovereign star
Smiling athwart the gloom of war!

IX

TRUCE.

Then Eben Stark and Kawanute
  With hand in hand fraternal stood:
  And round them came their brotherhood —
The pale-face, and moccas'ined foot.

Each looks at each in wonderment
  And weird suspense... Enchantment strange!
  What sorcery hath wrought the change?
What power occult was hither sent?—

Dark eye and blue electric met
  In glistening flashes hence and thence:
  'T was LOVE—Earth's one omnipotence!—
And thine the magic, sweet brunette!

Is there no shadow lurking there
With scowling brow? Beware — beware!

Now down they sit on boughs of green —
  Pale-face and dusk- in council met,—
  Each takes in turn the calumet
In silence and in peace serene;
Their eyes on her, bright woodland lass!—
  Light as gazelle, and step as neat;
  Behind her fairy-skipping feet
Enamoured rose the supple grass.

A charm that lit her modest glance
  Lay mirrored in her lustrous eye,—
  A chaste and gentle sorcery
Kindled, illumined by romance.
  (Brighter the glance of Love may be,
  Darker the brow of Jealousy!)

The Pipe she brings the sachem grave,
  And next, in turn, each warrior bold —
  Like Hebe to the gods of old!—
A sweet solatium to the brave;
And each, while wreaths of azure rise,
Sends glance to her from tender eyes.

For Eben next the Pipe she lit,
　　With sweeter fragrance filled anew:
　　But sweeter, Eben thought, the dew
Her crimson lips had left on it!

He whiffs the graceful tortile rings,
　　And coronals of peace they rise
　　As if to crown and solemnise
A convocation of the kings!

On curling wings of blue depart
All evil spirits from the heart! *

X

OONAK—THE SILENT WARRIOR.

Not all are calm . . .
　　　　　　　　　　Not all sedate.
　　With sullen-leering eye is one
　　Among that score of warriors dun
Whose bosom flames in jealous hate,—

---

* "See, brothers! as a hawk flies up with a snake in his claws,
this smoke flies away with all bad thoughts of my heart."
　　　　　　—Holata-Ematila's *council speech.*

With darkling brow, foreboding threat,
  That warrior, Oonak, gloomed askance . . .
  How changed since leading in the dance
The light gazelle — the trim brunette!

Is this that silent warrior dark —
The foeman stern of Eben Stark?

———

'T was but a moon ago roamed he —
  With Onnalinda wandering
  Thro' wood and dell of daisied spring
And by the gladsome Genesee;
By cove and covert, brake and bower,
  They lingered in the starry dew,
  And often in their light canoe
They sailed till morning's rosy hour.

(Oh, Love!—thou strange anomaly!—
A nymph to smile on such as he!
'T is Beauty's freak:—Of old 't was said
That sooty Vulcan Venus wed.
Love winks at pranks and freaks like these,
And laughs at contrarieties.)

Sojourner he, and whence he came
A mystery he would not reveal;
Even Onnalinda's soft appeal
He answered curt:
              "Oonak my name,
Algonquin tribe."
                    So brusque, then mute.
Across the hills three moons ago
He boldly came with blade and bow,
And joined the braves of Kawanute.

When questioned else, he answered all
With "Ough "— a muttered guttural.
"Have you papoose or wife?"—asked she;
He answered "Ough," sepulchrally.
Then she, to banter: "When you come
To win a maiden, or to woo,
Suppose she answers 'Ough' to you?"
But Oonak sat as turtle dumb.
'T is he!—of whom she hinted —"brave
But silent as a forest grave."

She, jesting still so debonair:
"You ask, have I a pale-face swain,—
Suppose I answer so again!"
But dumb he sat, with sullen stare.

. . . With manly form, but eye of lynx;
Crafty but valiant; words but few;
And when they sailed in their canoe,
Bright prattler she, and he a sphinx.
Silence in love, forsooth, thought he,
Gave zest to its felicity.

XI

THE TUMULT.

The tale renew : —
                As Eben Stark
Smiling returned the calumet,
He kissed the hand of the brunette.
Behold! what flame from tiny spark:
As match to bomb — a mine it sprung! —
That kiss was torch to Oonak's rage.
He sprung! . . . His belt as battle-gage
At Eben's feet he fiercely flung!

Instant in camp confusion dire
Of threat and oath, of rage and scath,
Of eyes agleam 'neath brows of wrath —
A kindling red of surging fire.

Firm stood heroic Eben then
  While round him rose the baleful rage:

"Coward!" he cried: "I take the gage
And meet you where you will and when!
Is it to fright this tender maid —
  Is this a time for clownish fray?
  Base coward! come — I lead the way —
Take bow or blade to yonder glade!"

No coward Oonak. Flashed his look
  With rage, and hate's malignant glare.
  Then forth, as lions from their lair,
To ghastly glade their way they took.
  And following them, in solemn pace,
  Went Saxon band and dusky face.

Poor Onnalinda — stricken dove —
  Shrank trembling to her father's arm —
  But powerless he to quell the alarm —
The clashing feud of Hate and Love.
With hands upraised to tearful eyes
  The impending scene of death to dim,
  Pale Onnalinda followed him —
Beseeching him with sobs and sighs.

. . . The maddening flames of jealous rage
Ev'n Beauty's tears cannot assuage.

" Ho! warriors, cease!"
            The chieftain cried —
" What boots this wild uproar and brawl!
  My camp and court a carnival!
Who breaks this truce let woe betide!"

" Be calm, O chief!" said Eben brave —
" I know no truce in sight of shame;
  This lout, not I, must bear the blame;
And woe betide the boorish knave!
Hither I came from realm afar
  With worthy knights of brawn and brain;
  No record bleared with evil stain
Is ours, in council or in war.
This base intruder in your tribe
  Has flung his challenge at my feet;
  And here with blade his blade I meet,
With scorn his scoff, with taunt his gibe!
This damsel . . . worthy of her sire! —
  Bright fairy of the blooming glade!
  Her eye incites my eager blade
And lights my heart with wonted fire!

. . . No truce I break, save with yon knave
  Who brought the honoured Pipe to shame.
  Think you I crouch like dastard tame?
No! man to man, and glaive to glaive,
We twain shall end this craven feud
  Ev'n now, and here!"
                       He ceased.

                            With glance
  Of tiger Oonak glared askance
  Where Onnalinda shrinking stood.

  (One saw that glance. Did Ronald Kent
  Know it of old, and what it meant?)

Ah! who his dark intent could know?
  To mingle on the trampled sod
  His own and Onnalinda's blood
Ere he should fall by Saxon foe?
  Did Oonak fear the dire event—
  The risk of war's arbitrament?

Like panther fleet with fell design
  Sprang Oonak, darting to the maid,
  Whirling aloft his flashing blade—
A hideous ghoul incarnadine!

An instant hung that knife abhorred
  O'er swooning maid in terror bent
  When, PING!
        —a shot from Ronald Kent—
(Who trims the wing of humming-bird!)
The blade flew circling in mid air—
  Cut sheer from hilt in Oonak's hand:
  Astounded, chief and warriors stand,
And pale in mute amazement, stare.

Like gorgon dire with eyes of fire
Stands baffled Oonak in his ire.

XII

One moment in uncertain dread
  Confused they gaze; when lo! ... on all
  Amazement new and marvels fall
Like spectre sudden: A charging steed
Dashes amidst the startled throng!
  Reined by a maid of bearing high
  With fearless hand and flashing eye,
And Indian trappings round her flung.

Her glinting plumelet bowed and swayed
While charger pranced in proud parade.

One look she gave at Oonak grim,—
  He cowered in awe, as though her glance
  Transfixed his heart like glittering lance —
With words of scorn addressing him:

"Base traitor! . . .
        Vile and cruel knave!
  Think not I follow in your track
  To win a skulking traitor back:
I scorn you . . .
    Spurn you . . .
        Coward! — Slave!"

She paused. A silence deep . . . Like group
  Of figures cut in marble white
  They gaze on her with filmy sight,
While guilty eyes of Oonak droop.

———

What grace of movement and of mien!
  As queen upon her throne of state,
  She calmly on her palfrey sate,
And tranquil viewed the troubled scene.

Cool Ronald stood — so calmly proud,
Re-charging now his rifle true;
But once an upward glance he threw
To that bright plumelet as it bowed;
And she, that maiden, smiling sent
A brighter glance to Ronald Kent.

———

"On yonder hill" — (the maid renewed,
While Onnalinda, gazing mute,
'Twixt Eben Stark and Kawanute,
Flushed with reviving pulses, stood.)
"On yonder hill I lost my way.
I came from mighty tribe afar.
My comrades few, are knights of war.
We roamed in joust and in foray
To this sweet dale of daffodil.
... This morn from camp, alone I rode,
And heedless strayed thro' fragrant wood,
And lost my way.
From yonder hill
I saw the strife, I knew the cause,—
My heart, inured, quick told me this:
Wherever is evil, OONAK IS;
Wherever is sorrow, OONAK WAS.

Hither on wingèd steed I flew,
  And, swiftly nearing, soon I saw
  The deadly feud, the wild fracas,
And rescue shot from rifle true."

(She smiled at Ronald, and it gave
  His cheek a tinge of sudden bliss;
  ... What thing on earth so bright as this:
A glance of Beauty on the Brave!)

Then turning to chief Kawanute,
Proudly she spoke, and resolute;
And he, proud Iroquois, gave ear
To her whose tribe he scorned to hear;
For as the Greeks warred epic Troy
The Algonquins warred the Iroquois:

" Daughter am I of chieftain brave
  Of the Algonquin tribe afar;
  This Oonak named me 'Glinting Star'
When he to me this wampum gave,
Which now beneath his feet I fling,
  To make fit nest for rattlesnake
  Like grovelling Oonak, who would make
My heart a nest for ravaging.

" He would not woo like noble brave —
    With tender words and gallant deeds;
    But with his wampum-trinket-beads
His passion sought to win a slave;
The sentry of my heart's stockade —
    Virtue —with guile he sought to entice,
    Then captive take, and sacrifice
All treasures in the palisade.

"A maiden's heart to him was not
    A rose to treasure sweet and pure;
    'T was but a lentil for a boor —
A garlic for a greedy sot.
The purity he dare not stain
    He sought to blast by chilling slight . . .
    My heart I keep from stain or blight
And pure it ever shall remain.
Beware of him when he is mute,—
'T is silence of the panther's foot !"

She drew the rein,—

                    Flung back her hair,
    At Oonak glanced with flashing eye,
    And finger pointing scornfully,
Repeating with impassioned air:

" Base traitor!—

       Vile, and cruel knave!
  Think not I follow in your track
  With tears to win a traitor back:
I scorn you . . .

       Spurn you . . .

          Coward! slave!"

The rein she drew,—

       Her palfrey flew,
  A thistledown before the blast.
  They gazed; but Ronald wondering cast
A look confused. . . .

      " Who *is* she—who?
O heart!"—he sighed.

      " What could it mean,
That glance of the Algonquin queen?"

And gazed he still with wondering eye
  Till, haply startled, soon he sees
  Her plume uplifted by the breeze
And far behind her palfrey fly;—

He starts as if from dreamy trance —
O Ronald!—Blessed circumstance!—

O happy chance! As forth he speeds,
　We follow in his path afar,
　Leaving the council stern of war
To judge of Oonak and his deeds;—
Whate'er the sentence, let it be
The knell of vile duplicity.

———

Ronald, he flies on eager feet
　To find the plume.
　　　　　　　　O happy wight—
　O blessed breeze that winged its flight! . . .
Or was it ruse of maiden sweet?

Her palfrey wheels. Ronald she sees.
　Had she forecast that he would come
　With knightly grace to find the plume?
O Love's arch ingenuities!

Slow she returns with downcast eye
　As if in search — as if inclined
　To find what she hoped *not* to find. . . .
O love — thou maze, thou Mystery!—
One word alone can compass thee:
　Incomprehensibility!

XIII

"GLINTING STAR" AND RONALD.

They meet. . . .
        He bows. . . .
                So sweet she smiles
His heart beats plaudits to the wind
That whirled her plume so far behind,—
He wished it whirled for miles, and miles!—
  To search with her thro' glen and grove,
  Thro' tangled copse, by tarn and cove.

(With LOVE to guide, in lovers' quest
The impossible seems always best!)

Forth Ronald by her palfrey strode.
  Strict search he feigned, and hoped that she
  Would, for the nonce, be blind as he!
And thro' the hazel-copse she rode:

Thro' dale and dingle, bush and brake,
  They wandered, loitering, down and back—
  But clear they kept from beaten track!—
Bright plumelet! was it for thy sake?

Then, gazing furtively around,
  He thought she knew he thought she knew
  Where lay the plumelet full in view,
And (feigned surprise!) the plume he found.

With tender hand he lifted it —
Proud badge! for knight a guerdon fit —
And, giving it with humble grace,
Closer he scanned her charming face;
Deep in her eyes' soft depths there shone
A light that kindled with his own;
And gazed he, mute and motionless,
Into those depths of tenderness.
. . . As one in silent revery
Gazes with absent, fixéd eye,
Striving to catch, in glimpses fleet,
Visions that rise in memory sweet,
So Ronald seemed, as tho' his gaze
Caught a bright glimpse of other days;
And thoughts of yore came thronging fast,
Filled with dim visions of the past.

She smiled . . . Her eyelids drooping meek —
Those long, dark lashes on her cheek—
And over her face there came and went
The reddening flushes turbulent,

As if her pulses sudden leapt,
Startled with thoughts that long had slept.

So strange that smile she feigned to hide
It told him all.
          "O heaven!" he cried —
"'T is she! 't is she!"
         And to his breast
Her yielding form he wildly prest!
And on his heart her face in tears
  Was smothered in a blest relief —
Her love unchanged thro' all the years,
  True daughter of the Algonquin chief!
That little girl — that bud maroon! —
Thro' years had grown, 'neath suns of June,
And now by Ronald's side she stood,
The rose, full-bloomed, of womanhood!
Up from those buried Junes arise
Thronging, a thousand memories;
Those far-off years when, captive, he
First drew her tears of sympathy;
That first long night of sobbing grief
In camp of the Algonquin chief;
That sweet relief when first he knew,
When he was crying, she cried too!

They thought of all those tender years
That rose in smiles to set in tears —
Bright skies of youth, with menace flecked,
They view in happy retrospect;
Dear days of old, when he would teach
   And she (bright pupil!) learned so well
She knew the sweetest part of speech,
   And read his heart ere she could spell!
Then, ah! those days that darker grew
With tears, to dim their sunny blue;
When that mute warrior's wily plot
   With hate and dark intrigue was planned;
And through th' Algonquin chief he sought
   By stratagem to win her hand.
—And ah! that night when last they met
   And all the pangs of sorrow knew:
When tears of blank despair beset
   The clinging anguish of adieu!

Thus Ronald and the Glinting Star,
   His only love — his first, his last —
   After the long, long years, o'ercast
With lowering clouds of dark despair,
So happily and so strangely there
   Meet in a fond embrace at last.

To them this recompense was given
  For that dark night of long ago —
When yearning gaze they sent to Heaven,
  Praying in agony of woe:
The rapture of that meeting there
Was the answer to their yearning prayer.

And now thro' hazel-copse they stray,
  In converse of the days gone by;
In gladsome mood they wend their way
  To yonder vine-clad canopy;
And there they sit, her hand in his,
Recounting wondrous histories
Of lives eventful. Happy twain! —
Who met — who parted — met again.

With eyes upturned inquiringly
To Ronald now, thus questioned she
Of scene so nigh a tragedy:

GLINTING STAR.

Who is the maid I saw to-day —
Whom vengeful Oonak sought to slay?

RONALD.

The chieftain's daughter —highborn maid.
Haply the ball outstript the blade!

GLINTING STAR.

Then she is not your sister?

RONALD.   Mine?

Would I could call the heroine
By name so tender. Sister? No.
Why ask me?

GLINTING STAR.

                    She resembles you —
A Saxon voice, a Saxon hue.

RONALD.   .

Oh, flattery! 'T would please a king
To be like her in any thing!
You saw our captain? He 'd forswear
His name, fame, all the world for her —
To be her humble worshipper!
Last night he told such tales I laughed,
And told him she would turn him daft!

He said she was of noble blood,
This pretty maiden of the wood!

GLINTING STAR.

She *has* a look, a gentle grace
Betokening a noble race.

RONALD.

Yes,—but he says this Indian girl
Can claim a grandsire in an earl!
Such claim what boots it to prefer
If earl shall make no claim for her?
What if I too should claim to be
Earl's grandson, and he claim not me!
. . . And then he prates of coronet
Where "pearls above the leaves are set,"—
A thousand such fantastic fancies
Flash thro' his brain from Beauty's glances . . .
You know the tale that, long ago,
At quiet eve I read to you —
An ancient tale of Love and Arms,
Of heroes bold and Beauty's charms:
A lovely nymph, who, in that age,
Set king and warrior in a rage —

The sovereign made her sweet alliance,
And set the warrior at defiance.
The hero flung his armour down —
He cared no more for king or crown —
That nymph was dearer than renown.
. . . A sounding tale; and tho' 't is true,
'T is nothing strange, and nothing new,
For here 's another tale of Troy—
Another nymph: that Iroquois!—
Our captain will aver that she is
A sweeter rose than loved Briseïs! *
He calls her, "Onnalinda sweet—
A paragon from face to feet!"

GLINTING STAR.

She 's charming . . .
            I have heard it said
That Saxons, rich and noble-bred,
Have images of such as she,
And hold them in idolatry.

RONALD.

Ah! you remember, long ago,
That little disk of cameo?

---

* " The loved Briseïs, like the blooming rose."
                    —ILIAD, **Book XIX**

Since that sad night you gave it me
Each day I 've blest you tenderly,—
You little knew the treasure hid
'Neath secret spring and tiny lid!

GLINTING STAR.

As keepsake of a last adieu —
'T was all I had — I gave it you.

RONALD.

You little knew its tiny space
Held worlds for me;
   A sweet, dear face!
Within my bosom, here, it lies
Sacred, unseen by other eyes.
Look! see you this?... its spring concealed...
Behold!—
  My mother's face revealed!

GLINTING STAR.

Sweet face! 't is like —

RONALD.

   —but, pardon me,
Whence came the disk? Who gave it thee?

GLINTING STAR.

'T was Oonak — when with bribery
And plot he sought to entangle me.
'T was found long years before, he said,—
'T was when you first were captive led.
'T was in a glade where hostile raid
Burst on our tribe from ambuscade ;
They captive seized a woman pale,
And hurried her o'er hill and dale.
Next day, in glade, upon the ground
That disk the dusky Oonak found.

RONALD.

My mother! O my mother! . . . Years
But sanctify that face with tears.

GLINTING STAR.

Her face — how strange. . . .

On closer view
Though it is like . . . yes, much like you,
'T is more like her I saw to-day
Whom cruel Oonak sought to slay —
Her you call "Onnalinda sweet."
Look ! . . .

Is the likeness not complete?

Ronald no answer made. He sate
  Gazing and pondering silently
As one who strives to read his fate
  In the dim blank of vacancy.

Long time his mother's face he viewed
  In revery and solicitude—
A vague suspense he could not hide
Though one beloved was by his side.

—Here leave the twain. We meet again.
Ah! may they be as happy then!
Our steps we turn—'t is drawing late—
We speed to learn of Oonak's fate.

XIV

OONAK.

Tho sun is low. . . .
        The winds are mute. . . .
  We near tho group in council met.
  By Eben sits the bright brunette,
And nigh them, judge-like, Kawanute.

In thongs of moose-bark, Oonak, bound,
  Before the judge shrinks glowering grim,
  While silent either side of him
The dusk- and pale-face gather round.

Rises the chief. His outstretched hand
  At Oonak points. A potentate
  With voice oracular, mien sedate:

"You man of lies!—
            Here bound you stand,
Like crouching dog red-stained with blood.
  By truth and law you have been tried—
  By truth and law which you defied.
Oonak! what now? Speak! if you would."

A guttural "*ough*" came his reply;
  And a scowling glance afar he sent
  Where Glinting Star and Ronald went,—
A fiendish vengeance in his eye.
Dumb Oonak! silence fits you well.
Dumb Oonak—sphinx inscrutable!
He who says aught when naught to say
May prattle when he ought to pray!

Indignant rose the chieftain's ire
And flashed his eyes' avenging fire,
As sternly to his braves he said:

"Take ye this Oonak forth straightway!
    If seen alive, hence from to-day,
Two of your lives are forfeited.
And ye—"
            —Here sudden the brunette
    Upon her sire laid gentle hand
    As if to break the stern command;
With tender voice, and dark eyes wet,
Some words she spoke in earnest plea
    That touched with light his brow of gloom—
    (A ray of hope for Oonak's doom?)
He paused . . . He stood reflectively,
Then spoke:
            "Bad Oonak! tho' you give
    No heed to woman's prayer or tear,
    Henceforth, I know, you'll hold them dear:
I speak—you die: She prays—you live!
Your life I spare. Quick, yonder go
    On foxes' feet!—no laggard pace—
    And join your vile Algonquin race
Afar beyond the Ontario . . .

Hold! . . . Ere you go, your ear I nick—
  Like white man's sheep—with forkéd ear
  I mark you well!
            Come no more here:
You come again, and die! Go—quick!"

(. . . If there's one man for Heaven unfit,
Truly, it is the Hypocrite!
. . . If one can merit a scourge inhuman,
'T is knave who wins and flouts a woman.)

———

Glowering around, with sullen tread
  Went Oonak on his lonely way.
  Night with her mantle dusk and gray
O'er wood and glade a glamour spread.

XV

While to the camp as firm allies
  Return the groups of either race,
  We follow Oonak's crafty pace,
Mistrustful of his vengeful eyes.

Lurking he went his devious way
  By reedy cove and covert dim;
  The lowering shades of night to him
Were goblin-wraiths that seemed to say:
" We 're ghosts of buried love ... We come
  To follow Oonak to his doom!"
Each swaying bough — a spectral shade —
To him a mock obeisance made.
Scowling he went his darkling way,
  Cringing at phantoms rising grim;
  Till halting short, . . . as if to him
A demon shrieked a sudden stay!
With quivering palm above his eyes
  Around he scowled with fiendish glare,
  Then from his path struck angular.
On stealthy step and dark emprise
Skulking he went. With lurid face
  Cadaverous in the moon's wan ray,
  Like cougar creeping to his prey
Crept Oonak on his crafty pace.
With wary hand each twig and bough
  He parts. He creeps on bended knee.
  He halts . . . He listens . . .
                    Can it be
The hum of breeze — or voices low?

Is it some happy rural swain
  Who wanders hither with his love
  To linger in the hazel-grove
'Neath happy stars?—Ah! hapless twain!

Near and more near, and stealthier yet
  Crouching he creeps on quivering knee.
  On yonder vine-clad canopy
His gloating tiger-eyes are set.

A voice he hears that from afar
  Recalls the tender days of old,
  Ere love too bold grew harsh and cold—
Chilling the heart of Glinting Star.

(. . . Ah! maiden of the rosy lip:
  A swain loves most when most in doubt,—
  Keep him just NEAR, AROUND, ABOUT;
We firmest hold what seems to slip.
. . . Would you a lover fervent keep?
  Oft let love's fire burn low and faint,—
  Beneath the ashes of restraint
Subdue its flame, and let it sleep.)

Oonak a jewel would not prize
Until 't was dear to other eyes:
And as he saw her love expire
His love arose in maddening fire!

Listening . . .

        Halting . . .

                He creeps along . . .
Again that voice!—a tender cry —
A wail of wakened memory;
It is a maiden's tender song:

1

Calm as the night
  Was heart of mine,
Lulled in the light
  Of day's decline.
No breezes stirred
  The folded wing
Of dreaming bird
  Soft slumbering,
Like heart of mine —
  O heart of mine!

2

Love came and broke
  The slumber deep —
The bird awoke
  From happy sleep,
Ruffled its wing
  In wild unrest —
A cruel sting
  Was in its breast,
Like heart of mine —
  O heart of mine!

Then ceased the tender song; but soon
Is heard a voice of deeper tone.

XVI

THE ENCOUNTER.

Now flames grim Oonak in his ire!
  Another voice! Calm voice and low,—
  And can it be his hated foe?
The thought turns all his frame to fire!

Sudden he rises . . .
                  Close is he
Upon the vine-clad canopy.

He leaps—he springs like beast of prey.
  He fiercely clasps his foe around!
  Clenched fast they fall upon the ground.
They struggle wild in deadly fray . . .

Ronald—'t is he!
                  Keen Oonak found
The prey he tracked like subtle hound.
O hapless maiden—Glinting Star!
  Of no avail thy shriek and wail;
  And Ronald's aim of no avail—
To trim the wing of bird afar.

Wan faces 'neath the ghastly moon
  Grin fiendish.
           Grasped in deadly clench,
With grappled forms they yerk, they wrench,
They turn, they roll, in struggle prone.

Ah! Ronald—what a change is come
  From tender dalliance soft and sweet!
  And, waning Star!—God help thee meet
Perchance thine own and Ronald's doom.

Impetuous strife in even scale:
  They pause . . . They breathe . . .
            They close again.
  They roll, they writhe, they strike, they strain.
Midst groans are heard the maiden's wail.
Faint with the terrors of the fray
She shuddered, moaning in dismay.

Hard pressed is Ronald—sinking fast,
  The ogre Oonak o'er him lies
  With rigid grasp and flaming eyes,—
Ah! must brave Ronald yield at last?
Her cry he hears!—His arm he wields—
If yield he must, to Death he yields!

That shriek of maid nerves every limb!
His thews give quick convulsive throo!
He springs—he whirls the fiend below!
. . . And Oonak sinks aghast and grim.

—So ends that warrior's dark career.
Held firm to earth he silent lies.
And all is silent save the cries
Of stricken maid in shuddering fear;
These die away in quivering moan
Like evening breeze's dying croon.
And Ronald now with hunting-blade
Takes trophy from his vanquished foe—
Grim souvenir—in proof to show
The fate of Oonak, renegade!

Brave Ronald and the Glinting Star
Thro' moonlit copse now wend their way,
Whither they hear her palfrey neigh
Recall for her—the wanderer.
In balmy dale they linger long:
And hearts that quailed in dire distress
Now peaceful beat in tenderness—
Soft rhythmed like a gentle song.

—Return we now to camp afar.
  The hours flit by in happy flight.
  A benison and a kind good-night
To Ronald and the Glinting Star!

XVII

THE CAMP.

Eben awakes . . . Alert is he
  Tho' all the camp in slumber lies;
  While purple tints—Hope's auguries!—
Gladden the Vale of Genesee,
  Whose river in clandestine Grove
  Kisses the waters of the Cove.

And smiling wakes vermilion Morn—
  Tingeing the east with crimson blush;
  The bobolink and busy thrush
Make wild with song the blooming thorn.

And busier yet the camps awake
  While jubilant reveille sounds;
  Each warrior from his pallet bounds
To greet the radiant morning break.

Gayer than wont, and scrupulous
  This morn is Eben in his dress;
  His comrades hint of "daintiness"
And smile with ogles ominous.

A WORD ASIDE.

A moment here the scribe would break
The story's thread, for Eben's sake —
A word aside, in lower tone
And, bracket-bound, for him alone.
Reader! pass on, 't is not for you —
Unless like Eben a lover too! —

[O'erweening Eben! be not sure:
Possession, only, is secure.
Think not her smile 's convincing sign —
A proof — that Onnalinda 's thine.
'T were pert to cite, in flippant phrase,
A screed on woman, and her ways,
But over your door put Motto-scrip —
Or picture — of "the cup and lip."
. . . But, courage! swain — if woman CAN,
She surely WILL NOT flout a man.
But be not sure! — tho' she may cry,
There 's mischief twinkling in her eye.

A riddle Samson could not solve:
  Her "no yes no"—her "yes no yes."
The **Stagirite** could not resolve
  This charming sphinx of rebuses!
Each word abetted by a glance
Pierces his thesis swift as lance,—
Quick as Apache spears his victim
She stabs his predicated dictum.
So, Eben Stark, beware! beware
Of woman's ways so debonair!
She sets a-flame with sparkling eye
The Stoic's cold philosophy;
Maudlin is he in tenderness
O'er thread that trails behind her dress;
Ecstatic on a burr he'll dote
If plucked from hem of petticoat;
And many a brave Rinaldo yet
Is tangled in Armida's net.
At times she'll teach that love Platonic
Is worse or better than love Byronic.
To man it seems caprice—a whim—
When half the foible is in him:
What he'd have HER, that *he* must BE—
Be each to each auxiliary,—
As Socrates was no gallant
Xanthippe turned a termagant.

. . . O woman! what a guy to *her*
The scientist or philosopher!
Do you believe Pythagoras —
   That as some beast we lived erewhile —
She 'll grant perchance you were an ass,
   A guinea-pig or crocodile:
She 'll recognise *your* ancestry,
But claim no consanguinity!
And would you ask, "What think you, madam,
   Of Evolution, now in vogue —
   Molecular germs in dust or fog?"
She 'll say, "My primal sire was Adam,
   Perhaps yours was a polliwog!"
She 'll trace her genealogy,
And let him trace his own, you see.
. . . Such theories are to her as chaff—
She blows them with a rippling laugh.
The buddhist, atheist, and gnostic,
   The deist and iconoclast,
Beneath her searching, scorching caustic
   Wriggle and twist like worm aghast.
Their premise, smiling she 'll admit,
   Then with one word, and eyes a-bright'ning,
She gives their syllogism a fit—
   They think it struck with bomb or lightning!

. . . Beware, O Eben! woman's eyes
Still lure a thousand Antonies,
And half mankind is still beset
With Cleopatras of brunette!
If woman's not a Rosalind
  And Portia and Imogen —
The Sweet, the Pure, the True, combined,—
Such you will find her ere you find
  One Phocion 'mong a million men.
—Man is an eagle flying high;
  Small things he scorns, or sees not any;
Woman's a chickadee close by,
  And sees each speck, each rift and cranny.
. . . O woman! wisest, brightest, best!
Knows all man knows—she'll guess the rest!—
Knows all man knows, and in addition,
Knows every thing by intuition.
And be she aborigine,
  Or Saxon blonde, or arch brunette,
She'll teach a man in love that he
  Not even knows his alphabet!
——Ah, sanguine Eben! be not sure;
Your bond's yet blank — lacks signature!—
Possession, only, is secure.]

XVIII

ONNALINDA ARRAYED.

The tale renew:—
　　　　From flitting dreams
　Wakes Onnalinda—charming lass!—
　Like glistening dew upon the grass
Sparkle her eyes with radiant beams.

Her lissom form in soft attire
　She trimly robes with dainty hand,
　And decks with princess' ermine grand—
Rich trophies won by hunter-sire,
Richer than purple garb of Tyre!

Her fairy feet in chamois shoon
　With jet and amber beads begemmed;
　Her shapely waist bright diademmed
With sheeny circlet—starry zone!
　On rounded arm an amulet;
　A chaplet o'er her brow she set;
In opulence her lustrous hair,
Faint-scented with aroma rare,
　Fell round her form. . . . O sweet brunette!

Bright is the day! The thronging birds
  Bibble and babble songs ecstatic,
  Like poet in a fit erratic
Metering, jingling, jargon words.

The quiet waters of the Cove
  Lie as if dreaming sweet and calm;
The boughs of bloom bend from above
  With solace of ambrosial balm.
O'er glimmering vale, and lazy dune
Quivers the lambent air of June.

No hut of Celt, or Saxon pale,
  Then broke the landscape's harmony—
No hovel flecked this emerald vale
  Like mote in Beauty's azure eye.

No Slanderer then, with tongue of asp,
  Darted his slime at each fair name;
No Gossip fouled with slimy grasp
  The roll of Virtue and of Fame,—
The Slanderer then was in his cell
Deep in the Ninth * foul cave of hell.

* INFERNO, Canto xxx

XIX

Forth to the mead leads Kawanute;
  Bright Onnalinda by her sire;
  Eben and band in gay attire;
Then warriors of moccas'ined foot.
. . . Fantastic troop!—a motley train,
Surging and winding o'er the plain:
The Saxons white, in coats of blue,
Marching aligned in order due;
Red warriors striped with every tint
Of plant or berry, scoke or mint;
Mantled in garb of gayest tinge;
Leggings of doe with quill and fringe;
All tasselled and plumed, before, behind,
With feathers waving in jocund wind!
Onward they went, of every hue,—
Grotesque that motley retinue!

"... I know you, Eben Stark, and well"—
  Said Kawanute the sachem grave—
"And well I know the Saxons brave,
With eyes of hawk. My warriors fell

Before your aim. We held our breath,—
We knew that Eben Stark was Death!"

"Brave Kawanute!"—then Eben said—
  "We raise no more the bow or brand:
  I come to claim—to ask—the hand
  Of ONNALINDA—woodland maid!"

"How can she be so dear to you—
    Does pale-face love so soon—so soon?
And how can Onnalinda know
    You love so quick—one moon, one moon!
Bad love is quick, and swift of foot:
Quick come—quick go!"—says Kawanute.

"He that would run with laggard pace
    With such a guerdon as the prize—
Love that would loiter in the race
    Beneath bright Onnalinda's eyes—
His feet are lead; his soul is dark;
His eyes are blind!"—says Eben Stark.

KAWANUTE.

Where have the Saxon maidens fled?—
Will not the pale-face daughters wed?

EBEN STARK.

The Saxon maid? There's naught can vie
With the heavenly azure of her eye,
But dark eyes dart a lance as bright
As lightning-rift athwart the night!
. . . Brunette's a ruby; blonde's a pearl:
But blonde's a saint,—brunette's a girl!

KAWANUTE.

Hold! hold!—what 's ruby, blonde, and pearl,
Lances and lightning, saint and girl?
When Indian jingles words so bad,
We Indians call him crazy-mad!
When white man 's mad, and dares to show it,
They say you white men call him "poet"!—
They jingle talk,—I see that you
Try fly sky-high as poets do!

EBEN STARK.

No poet I,—plain "Eben Stark."
I 'd be a loon, and not a lark!
Tho' poets great, unlike the player,
Grow greater as they 're growing grayer,
Small poets early cease their song
And rhymes grow short as beards grow long!—

They cease to soar — on earth they tarry —
The lark turns loon, and —

KAWANUTE.

— then they marry!

Merrily rose a peal of laughter,
Echoing thro' the woodlands after.
Onward, as if on project bent,
Both pale and dusky warriors went
Together o'er the daisied plain;
　But Onnalinda, Eben Stark,
　And Kawanute the sachem dark,
In earnest council here remain.

XX

A QUESTION.

The chieftain now, with lifted brow,
　Turned to the princess, speaking grave:
"My Onnalinda!—when, and how,
　And where met you this Saxon brave?
A mystery to me, it seems
Hid in the foggy land of dreams."

A tinge carnelian flushed her cheek
As Onnalinda answered meek:

XXI

ONNALINDA EXPLAINS.

"One afternoon, ere twilight's hour,
    I wandered from my little tent
    And far into the woodlands went,
Led by the charm of bird and flow'r;
    June's breath around me, and above
    Carolled the happy songs of love.

"Only my heart foreboding beat—
    Was it a shadow crossed my way?
'Has Evil found this blest retreat?
    Beware !'—my timorous heart would say.
And yet my feet prest onward still
Heedless of omen good or ill.

"Far down the river from this Cove,
    A little brook in babbling glee
    Leaps laughing to the Genesee;
And there, within a lovely grove,
    I sat, while birds a music made
    Sweet as pale lover's serenade."

[She paused a breath. She smiled to see
Eben grow flushed at flattery
So subtle; he was ne'er endued
With voice of bulbul.

              She renewed :]

"While thus I lingered in the nook
Listening to song of bird and brook,
Far in the woods the sudden sound
   Of crackling bush quick broke the charm.
   Startled I rose in dread alarm,
When, past me with a vaulting bound,
Darted a doe and then a hound.
   Into the river deep the doe
   Leapt, plashing, from its howling foe.
Trembling I gazed.

             Then peering through
   The covert where I shrinking stood,
Two braves I saw, in caps of blue,
   Come swiftly thro' the crackling wood.

"They halted by my covert near
   Where close concealed I trembling lay;
Their hurried breathing I could hear;
My heart seemed throbbing in my ear—
   A traitor ready to betray.

They stood, and watched the doe at bay,
  (Their rifles resting on the ground,)
They seemed in pity for the prey
  Harassed with menace of the hound.
Pale-faces they; and though equipped
  With pouch and horn and hunter's knife,
Their coats and caps with tinsel tipt
  Gave token of the warrior's life.
The one a chieftain, proud and tall,
Who called the other, 'corporal.'

" I gladly heard the gallant chief
  Speak tenderly of harassed doe;
He little knew what blest relief
  He gave to one in covert low!

" 'Call off the hound!'
           The chief he cried —
'Such cruel sport I will not bide, —
No hunter worthy of the name
Will slay the snared, defenceless game, —
Call off the hound!'
           Such tenderness
Gave solace to my heart's distress.
Brave chief! with sympathy inspired —
Whom first I feared, I now admired.

"Soon up the bank the obedient hound
Darted, trail-sniffing, round and round,
Scenting and prowling—forward and back,
Sniffing and howling—a new-found track!
Near me and nearer at each bound,
Circling my covert round and round;
Near me and nearer, till at my side . . .
'Save me! oh save!'—I shrieking cried.
Quick sprung the hunter to my aid;
Amazed but calm of voice he said:

"'Fear not—fear not, my pretty maid!
Safe are you here from hurt or harm
As though upon your father's arm.
. . . Why came you to this lonely glen?'

"Meekly I told him why, and when.
I told my name, my home; and then,
(Grown braver 'neath his cheery smile,)
Of sire, of camp, of Cove, and isle.
His comrade—worthy to be his peer—
Now spoke to him in undertone,
Then turned, a distant sound to hear,
And followed hound and flying deer,—
The chief and I were left alone.

His voice and face, of guile so free,
His kindly smile and courtesy,
A sweet assurance gave to me.

" He told me of his home afar,
   And how he joined with France—our foe;
The unholy strife he did abhor;
And, wearied with the wicked war,
   He came to hunt the bounding doe.
He told of comrade-braves — a score,
   Who came with France's marshalled men,
But left the ranks. They war no more —
   They hunt the deer awhile, and then
On Kadaracqui's peaceful shore
   With him they greet their homes again.

" Their tents are pitched at Crooked Bow,—
   Methinks I 've heard their distant drum,—
A sprightly oar in light CANOE
   In little hour may go and come ! "

[Pausing, she smiled. The sachem, he
   Wondered why she, and Eben too,
Should smile at mention of CANOE !
Demurely then continued she:]

" Strange tales he told . . .

                 An hour flew by,
And sunset tinged the evening sky.
Bewildered now I sought the trail
That homeward led thro' bush and dale.
The pale-face chief before me went
    Parting the boughs that interlace,
     Till, gazing thro' an open space,
Afar I saw our island tent.
He stood; then spoke so tenderly:

"'When far away I know I'll meet
    In fairy dreams a princess sweet—
    Her name shall ONNALINDA be!'

" He bowed. He waved his cap of blue,
And tenderly he said, 'Adieu!' . . .
A deep regret was in that tone,—
    It seemed a sigh or tear repressed,
A veil seemed o'er my senses thrown—
    Thro' misty eyes my path I guessed.
. . . As wounded starling to its nest
Flutters with sorrow in its breast,
With fluttering heart I homeward drew,
Touched with the sorrow of adieu."

And Onnalinda paused.

        Then he,
Her noble sire, with brows relent
As if in kind encouragement,
  With gentle voice inquiringly:

"You met but once? How can you know
  He 's not our foe in crafty guise—
  These braves who come in quick surprise
How know you they are not our foe?"

Mystic, but meekly, answered she:
 "Each eve I wandered from my tent
  I knew not how or why I went—
A woodland fairy beckoned me.
I know a spirit led my way,
And such a guide will not betray;
I found, whatever path I took,
My heart before me at the brook!
Each eve I saw, when gazing through
  The covert where I lingering stood,
One pale-face, in his cap of blue,
  Come softly thro' the silent wood.
New tales and strange he told each day
Of sights and cities far away;

Of battles, sieges, fort, and trench,
Of Saxon struggles with the French.
And then, with sadness in his eye,
He told of peril drawing nigh:
There came, he said, ev'n yesterday
Command from Denonville, it read:

"'Quick join the ranks! One hour delay,
I come and take you, 'live or dead!'

"'T was answered: 'Threats are empty wind.
Send me no more your lackeyed hind.
We war no more with Kawanute.
We hunt the doe,—but not too blind
To see a Frenchman or to shoot!'"

At this her sire in laughter broke,
And gayly, in acknowledgment,
A smile and nod to Eben sent.
And then in thoughtful mood he spoke:

"How came these braves?—Who was their guide?
If friends why come in quick surprise
With rifles aimed by eagle eyes?"
Then Onnalinda shrewd replied:

"In arms they came to prove to you
  Their courage and their kindness too;
Their rifles keen showed kind intent —
Prepared for war is to prevent.
They took you by a quick surprise
To prove the white man swift and wise.
A spirit led them on their way
Who led ME to the nook each day!
Could not a spirit guide thro' wood?
  Or walk, or talk, or sail canoe?
What man can do a spirit could,
  And these a little maid can do!"

Her questions 'woke a droll surprise —
  The sachem's eyes in mist appear;
But brightly blinked the maiden's eyes
  At words she spoke for Eben's ear!
The sachem pondered — fogged in doubt,—
  WHAT spirits walk and talk and do?
He seemed the most perplexed about
  The spirit sailing in canoe!
. . . As when three gossipers are heard,—
  The first one something strange has said;
The second, sly, winks at the third;
  That means: "You know him—wrong in head."

So winked the sachem—as much as said,
"A little flustered in her head!"
But still he knew her logic good:
"What maid can do, a spirit could!"
Though dazed, and darkly mystified
With Onnalinda's spirit-guide,
Her filial truth he would believe —
So guileless she could not deceive,
Good ghosts, he said, were never about
    When HE went groping the thickets through!
"If spirits would guide the white man out
    They 'd surely guide old Indian too!..."
And still it was his darkest doubt
    Of spirits a-paddling in canoe!

———

Tarrying thus in colloquy
    On themes of strange concern intent,
    Sudden they turn in wonderment. . . .
Approaching, who are these they see?

A maid, a palfrey, and a groom!
    Advancing near, they recognise
    And cheerily greet with glad surprise
Ronald, and maid with flowing plume.

XXII

DISCLOSURE.

In Ronald's face they well might see
A look of weird perplexity.
And scarce a greeting did he give,
But cast a look inquisitive,
Gazing at Onnalinda. . . . Why,
Why turned to her that troubled eye?
. . . Then touching Eben's arm, the two
From out the group apart withdrew
In low and hurried interview.

Meanwhile "The Star," in story brief,
Gave Onnalinda and the chief
A swift recital of events
  That seemed to them strange mysteries;
And, ere she paused, told incidents
  That startling 'woke a new surmise.
And when she paused, in mute suspense
  They gazed into each other's eyes.
Ronald and Eben — can we know
  What weighty theme engrosses them?
Is it some new discovered foe
  Lurking in plot and stratagem?

No. We shall guess,—when coming near,
Eben's last words we overhear:
"Yes, Ronald, so she said last night.

   Would I had told you this before,
But since that hour, in bustling plight
With hurried march and threatened fight,
   I thought of it no more . . .
But there she is . . . Go, Ronald! go,
Ask Onnalinda—we shall know."

Pale with a deep anxiety
   Ronald before the maiden stood
Silent and motionless. And she
   Viewed him with faltering attitude,
As if both doubt and hope were blent
Into a vague presentiment,
That from the far-off years he came
   As messenger with tidings sweet,
And that he bore the tender name
   Her mother would so oft repeat.

Then Ronald from his bosom drew
   The disk—that face he loved so well—
And held it open to her view
   While tears, repressed, his eyelids swell.

A sudden pallor blanched her cheek.
She started with a tremulous shriek:

"Mother!—
  My mother's face!—
    'T is she! . . .
Ronald! O Ronald!—
    It is he! . . . "
That disk—that face beloved so well—
She clasped with eyes to Heaven, and fell
In Ronald's arms, and sobbed, "My brother!"
 And in his loving arms he pressed
 His own sweet sister to his breast,—
The children of one sainted mother.

 ("Half-brother," him the world would deem,
 But brother in her heart's esteem.)

    ———

 The scene we leave to painter's skill—
Beyond the touch of poet's quill:
The blank amaze of noble chief
 Who oft the name of "RONALD" heard
When, years before, HER tears of grief
 Flowed at the mention of that word!

And now his rapturous delight —
   The disk that stirred fond memory!—
That face that beamed upon his sight,
   And moved to sacred ecstasy.
His frame was thrilled with tender joy—
Brave Kawanute, the Iroquois.

The Glinting Star and Eben stood
Gazing, but in no startled mood,
For well they cherished broad surmise
(Dulling the brightness of surprise)
That now, this hour, a glad event
Would thrill the heart of Ronald Kent.

XXIII

Now arm in arm, thro' mead afar,
   Ronald and Onnalinda went,
While Eben, chief, and Glinting Star,
   Stood pondering o'er the strange event.

And need we ask where roam the two?
   Or ask what sudden thought first sent
   A thrill thro' heart of Ronald Kent
Tho' her he met he never knew?

Her face, her form, to him revealed
One whom the years and tears concealed.
Alas! till now one little ray
   Of hope he saw — so slight, but sweet —
That somehow . . . somewhere . . . in some way
   His long-lost mother he should meet.

'T was not to be.
             Across the mead,
By Onnalinda loving led,
He goes to yonder sacred glade
Where gentle hands a mound have made
Sweet with the rose and daisy blent;
   Under the bloom their mother sleeps,
   And there sad Onnalinda weeps,
And by her side kneels Ronald Kent.

Thus linger they an hour above
That hallowed shrine of mutual love.

Tho' in his heart deep sorrow dwelt,
Yet one dear solace Ronald felt:

His mother's path thro' all those years
Beamed with a love undimmed by tears.

When memories gloomed her heart in grief
It vanished 'neath the smile of chief,—
Deep in his heart and tenderly
Beloved, revered, adored was she.

And Ronald now that solace felt—
   The mist of years uplifted wide—
As by his mother's grave he knelt
   With Onnalinda by his side,
In whose sweet face there softly dwelt
   The loveliness of her who died.

Now arm in arm again they stray
   Across the sunny fields atar;
And sunnier, happier, Ronald's way
   When nearer to the Glinting Star!
. . . Again in joyous group they meet
   Around the chief in close attent—
Eben and " Onnalinda sweet,"
   The Glinting Star and Ronald Kent.

While thus their converse they renew,
   Across the dale we wander hence
   To that huge oak whose eminence,
As monarch, rules the distant view.

XXIV

THE RENDEZVOUS.

'T was noonday calm o'er mead and grove.
  Here stood that oak whose mighty form
  Was shield against both sun and storm,
And sentinel to isle and Cove.
Assembled 'neath the monarch tree
  Were groups of warriors tarrying,
Watching in bright expectancy—
  As vassals wait the approach of king.

Rifles and bows against the tree
Reclined in wondrous amity;
As if the Saxons' burnished arms
  Made friendly treaty with the bow,
  And these, in soft return, would show
Love for the Saxons' brilliant charms.

Here grouped a band of warriors dun,
  In garb of doeskin neat arrayed!
  And o'er their brows gay feathers swayed
Like bending lilies in lagune;
  Their garments edged with frill and fringe
  In pigments of the gayest tinge.

Sedate they sat in stoic ease
With arms a-kimbo round their knees,
Disdaining drill or order. Thus
They sat in group promiscuous.
And facing these, beyond the tree
A score of Saxon chivalry;
They stood in order's strict align
That showed their leader's discipline.
But why these clans in pomp compare?—
  As Beauty's self a fright would be
  Without the charm of modesty,
So warriors' pomp is tawdry flare
Without the thews to do and dare.

XXV

The meadow shone in velvet green,
With lace of daisies' silver sheen
  Brooched with the daffodils of gold,—
What 'neath heav'n's azure can compare
With that bright emerald robe so fair
  That God's own hand hath here unrolled! . . .
If He His footstool robes so bright,
What splendours crown His Throne of Light!
Sweet vale! unknown to ruthless band —
So pure, so fresh from God's own hand!

. . . Behold! thro' meadow's tender grass
  Comes one as tender, pure, and sweet;
  In chamois shoon so light her feet
The daisies smile — O winsome lass!
And by her side the chieftain dark,
  With stately step and kingly mien;
And on her right proud Eben Stark,—
  Bright Onnalinda walks between.
Behind them — on soft themes intent —
The Glinting Star and Ronald Kent.

They reached the groups beneath the tree;
  And Onnalinda's lustrous eyes
  Beam from their depths in gentle guise
To greet the Saxon chivalry.
They bend in homage, cap in hand,
  And greet her with a martial glance,
While rose the dusky warrior-band
  Bowing to her recognisance.

The chieftain standing 'neath the oak —
  Like it majestic and sedate —
  With pomp and grace of advocate
Thus grave but tenderly he spoke:

KAWANUTE'S ADDRESS.

"My children! hear me. I am old.
  My eyes are dim with dust of years.
Before me like a belt unrolled
  My path from youth to age appears.
—Before my path knew white man's foot
No sorrow knew old Kawanute.
The Frenchman came. . . . My path soon led
  Winding among my children's graves.
My heart was sore. The white man's tread
  Trampled the earth on buried braves.
. . . Shall foemen hurl us from this sod?
Our hearts lie under the sacred clod! —
That little grave by yonder tree
Holds all that made life dear to me!
. . . Glad, glad am I these Saxons here
Turn from the French to hunt the deer."

Then Kawanute with solemn tread
Turned to his dusky braves, and said:
"I fear no more this Saxon chief.
  These Saxon braves no more I doubt.
Too brave their chief for crafty thief —
  Brave heart within rules hand without.

"I 'll trust my Onnalinda's eye.
   If there 's a knave she finds him quick.
You know three moons ago a spy
   Sneaked to our camp as hunter sick.
In hunter's dress of fur and hide,
   With limbs so weak and joints so loose! —
We pitied as he groaned and sighed —
   We fed him as a sick papoose.
When him my Onnalinda eyed,
   With glance of peering chickadee
She saw straight through his dress of hide,
   And sent a warning glance to me.
Thro' rent in coat — a rift in seam —
   She saw a shining button gleam!
Danger he knew that glance did tell.
' Your meat' — he said — 'quick makes one well!'
He darted out. . . .
                Papoose so sick
Was never cured so sudden quick!"

The warriors laughed. But serious he
Continued in his dignity:

"As friends these Saxon braves have come, —
They hurl afar the Frenchman's drum.

Their chieftain wise and brave and kind,
  Will fight no more 'gainst Kawanute —
Will fight no more until too blind
  To see a Frenchman or to shoot!

" We bury tomahawk and bow;
  And he, — he buries gun and knife,
And asks that Onnalinda go
  With him on long-long trail of life."

XXVI

THE SURPRISE.

He scarce had ceased when — hark! . . .
                What sound
From woods that girt the meadow round?
Clamour of cries tumultuous swells —
Clamour of shouts and whoops and yells!
And louder, fiercer, wilder, higher,
Arose the fiendish yells, and nigher!
Around the mead for many a rood,
Wild uproar filled the trembling wood!
Up from the fen and glade and glen
Echoed the hillsides back again. . . .

Sudden from out the verge of wood,
Circling around for many a rood,
Savages wild in war-paint stood
   While shouts uproarious rent the sky!
Quick to their guns sprung Eben's troop,
Quick into marshalled order group,
Facing the storm of yell and whoop —
   Ready to do and ready to die!

"Comrades! let no ball miss its mark —
   Ready! Take aim!"—spoke Captain Stark.

"Hold! hold!"— Cried chieftain Kawanute —
"Would you my warrior-children shoot?"

Then high in air he raised his hand
As if afar to send command.
Instant a sudden silence fell
On all that fiendish whoop and yell;
As when the bellowing thunders cease
And all the land is hushed in peace.

Calm Eben stood, though in his eyes
A mingled look — not all surprise,
But wonder mingled with surmise.

He quick demanded:

              'Whence this crew
With whoop and howl and wild halloo!"

KAWANUTE.

Do you not see them quick obey
A sign from me! My warriors they!

CAPTAIN STARK.

If this be snare and stratagem
I answer not for you nor them.
And she. . . .

           I see her crafty smile. . . .
Am I ensnared by woman's guile!
And you I deemed to fealty true—
Is this foul treason planned by yon!
—I fear not all your savage rout
Tho' hills would shake with whoop and shout!

KAWANUTE.

A traitor I! . . .

          And *she* a cheat—
She who was "Onnalinda sweet!"

CAPTAIN STARK.

Think you your game so easy won!
Not till this mead with blood shall run,

And many a carcass lying low,
Food for the buzzard and the crow!
Ere comes that rabble here, the mead
Shall reddened be with swaths of dead!
My comrades few, but where we fall
Death shall hold gory carnival!
—Comrades! . . . Attention! . . . Ready—

KAWANUTE.

Hark—

Hear me a word, brave Captain Stark:
Do you forget that it was thus
Your white-face warriors came on us—
And as we 'woke, ere rising sun,
At each of us a levelled gun?
We Indians learn from white man quick,
And now, you see, we play you trick!
—But what did Onnalinda say,
To make excuse for trick you play
Ere break of day, with stealthy tread—
What was it Onnalinda said?

ONNALINDA.

I said he went to prove to you
His Courage and his kindness too:

To meet in arms a chieftain bold
Truly his dauntless Courage told;
Those rifles aimed, a kindness meant —
Prepared for war is to prevent.
. . . He took you by a swift surprise
To prove the white man swift and wise! —
To win your favour he would prove
His Courage, kindness, and —

CAPTAIN STARK.

     —his love!

KAWANUTE.

Give me your hand, brave Captain Stark! —
I too have proved you well! —

     Now mark:
These thousand braves who hem us round
Are warriors of my tribe renowned —
Beyond "The Cove" their camping ground.
Orders I sent them that with speed
They fill the woods around the mead;
'T was trick of mine; and you can tell
Whether I proved your courage well, —
Perhaps you heard my children yell?

—At this a peal of laughter broke;
Blue caps and feathers swung in air;
In triumph waved the monarch oak,
And hill and dale exulting 'woke
To join the jocund clamour there.
And higher, louder than before,
The savage shouts, in wild uproar
Like blatant trumpets, blare.
Sudden it ceased. . . .

Who comes apace
From yonder wood across the mead?
Two warriors of the dusky race —
And whom between them do they lead?
—Nearer they come. And now we see
His pale sad face. A captive he?
Surely a wight in woful strait,
Shuffling, footsore, on hobbling gait.

. . . "Ouf! merci!" . . .

Limping sore, he groans,
His half-shod feet on flinty stones;
Chapeau all torn to many a shred,
That hung like ringlets round his head;
Tattered his trousers, from the knees
Dangled the frills that flout the breeze;

Buttonless coat!—'t is held together
By grass and fern in twisted tether.
Sad eyes!—upon the ground they rest,
And heavy his chin upon his breast.
And see! his face and hands are torn
As if he came thro' briar and thorn!
. . . A rueful sight!

             A closer view:
What! is it he whom once we knew
With jewelled fingers, dainty wrist,
And sleek mustache to twirl and twist!
Lo! is it he—that man of note,
With manners sleek as was his coat!
A weird and marvellous change was this
As butterfly to chrysalis!

A burst of laughter, first from Donald,
Followed by Eben Stark and Ronald,
Then comrades all, till whoop and shout
'Woke woods with laughter round about!

. . . The FRENCHMAN! Tho' unbidden guest
In garb uncouth, he 'd be polite!
  He bowed, and then with hearty zest
  He joined the laugh, while many a jest
Made merry over the battered knight.

Gladly he saw that tartan stripe
That once he held in loving gripe,
When swift he fled, for life and limb,
From bogle, whoop, and horrors grim.
Little he thought that frank, broad face
Of Donald could writhe in mock grimace!
For still he thought that terrible night
Donald more crazed than he with fright!
. . . And now, as one from burning deck
Leaps gladly from the flaming wreck,
So he from whoop and horrors grim
Thankful escapes with life and limb!

His captors told:

　　　　　"In jungle thick
We found him, lost, and tired, and sick,—
And this. . . ."

　　　　　They handed to the chief
A missive with a message brief,
And fearless writ in bold relief.

Eben, he smiled with sparkling eye,
　And sly to Onnalinda bowed.
The chieftain, beckoning, called her nigh,
　To make the "paper talk aloud."

And Onnalinda broke the seal,
And read:

"*To Monsieur Denonville,—*
Your threats are but as blustering wind.
  I war no more with Kawanute.
We join your ranks when we 're too blind
  To see a Frenchman, or to shoot.
Sharp-shooters we—all men of mark—
  You 'll find us so.
            Yours,
                Eben Stark."

Uproarious laughter burst in air,
Followed by thousand shouts afar,
For well those braves, afar and near,
Knew when in gamesome mood to cheer.
Smiled Kawanute, while all the group
Gave merry laugh and jocund whoop.
With hand paternal on Eben's head,
  And smiling still, the chieftain said:
"'Sharp-shooter,' good!—you hit the mark!
Give me your hand, brave Captain Stark!"

Then Kawanute, as if to call
Attentive ear of warriors all,

His patriarchal hands outspread
Above the listening group, and said:

"My children! — Warriors of the bow.
   My brothers! — Warriors of the gun.
This gallant captain well you know
   Worthy to be a chieftain's son.
If there is here a voice of doubt,
I ask it, let it now speak out! . . .
No word. . . . I ask again, shall he
The guide of ONNALINDA be
On the long trail?"

         The woods awoke —
An echoing shout exultant broke,
That shook the boughs of monarch oak;
And ever answered as before
The shouts afar in clamorous roar, —
No languid call, or bravo tame,
Of opera lord or jewelled dame,
But like beleaguered city's cheer
Hailing its bold deliverer!

With timid glances, coy and shy,
Drooped gentle Onnalinda's eye.

The chieftain and old warriors dark
Smiled greeting to brave Captain Stark;
But hidden tears of deep regret
The younger warriors' eyelids wet,—
Their loss in vain they strove to hide;
Smiling they gazed, but smiling sighed!

XXVII

OSSEOLO.

One gallant youth, whose manly form
Ne'er trembled 'neath the battle storm —
Whose dark eye dared the fiercest foe
Nor quailed before his bended bow,
Now lowly gazed with dewy eyes,
Assuaging sorrow with his sighs.
The Princess he revered as one
　So far above his lowly sphere,
Like votary he gazed upon
　Her lovely face but to revere.

One eve, in the round moon of May,
　Forth to his little lodge she went,
　Where, wounded in fierce tournament,
This youth, young Osseolo, lay.

Across his throbbing brow her hand
　So softly, tenderly, she drew;
　It cooled his brain like falling dew
Upon a parched and feverous land.
As lily over the river's brim
　Bends low its form of gentle grace,
Bent Onnalinda over him —
　So near to his her lovely face!
She called him her "sick Indian brave"
　In tones of pity's tenderness;
And as she rose she turned and gave
　His burning brow a silent kiss.

. . . That night he dreamed that he became
A Saxon prince of knightly fame,
And wooed and won the heart and hand
Of loveliest princess in the land;
And "Onnalinda — princess sweet!"
Her name in dreams he would repeat.

Even the dusky one may dare
To woo, in dreams, a princess fair.
— Brief was his sunny dream of joy.
He wakes. . . . Ah me! poor Indian boy.
His dazzling dream, like meteor bright,
Flashed by, and darker was the night!

One boon he keeps: That eve in May
Those flowers she brought when ill he lay,
Now withered tuft that told a tale —
Dead daffodils and daisies pale.
—Ah! turn we from the unhappy lot
Of Osseolo. Blame him not
If hidden tear now dimmed his eye —
If in his heart a struggling sigh.
Nor princess Onnalinda blame,—
Perchance unconscious of his flame;
Burning unseen how could she know
The covered embers' fervid glow?
. . . Ye swains! so tender, shy, and mute—
In war or love be resolute!
Love's fortress would you have surrender?
Ask gently bold, and bravely tender!

XXVIII

EBEN AND ONNALINDA

Near Onnalinda Eben stood
  With martial mien and bearing high —
  The kindling glances of his eye
Bespoke his heart in happy mood.

But Onnalinda seemed to be
  By thoughts both sweet and sad beset.
  As though both gladness and regret
Were striving for the mastery.
Her sire, the chieftain, stood sedate,
  Gazing in Eben's manly face —
  Pleased by alliance with a race
Of proud demean and high estate.
  If in his heart regret could be
  'T was hidden 'neath stoic dignity.

One look to Heaven he gave to invoke
  The One Great Spirit of the sky,
  Then with a calm paternal eye
And voice of majesty he spoke —
  Raising with kingly sway his hand
  As if a silence to command:

"You, Eben Stark!
              The old sachem hear:
  I know you brave . . . I think you true;
  Else why could I now give to you
What is to Kawanute so dear?
  Dearer than my old heart to me —
  Dearer than all this earth is she;

She leads me to the grave where lies
One who had Onnalinda's eyes;
Whose gentle hand would lead me through
  Dark ways where oft I could not see.
May Onnalinda be to you
  What her sweet mother was to me!
Take her! . . .

      My poor old heart goes too! . . .
May the Great Spirit with you be!"

With tender grace chief Kawanute
  Placed Onnalinda's gentle hand
  In Eben Stark's. Each warrior band
Uprose with cheer and glad salute.

Mingled in amity, each race
  Gave hearty greetings. Ronald gave
  A gift unique to Eben brave
That brought amazement to each face;
At sight of it each heart beat quick,
  Till solving all its aim and drift
  They blest the fear-dispelling gift:
A dusky ear with dainty nick!
  Grim souvenir! but a potent charm
  'Gainst stealthy step and dire alarm!

The courier, now grown merry too,
Joined gayly in the brisk ado —
Stood proudly up in tattered coat
Like gamin of the "sans culotte;"
Thro' rag and rent he 'd show the grace
And port consummate of his race.
Scorning to be behind the rest,
He drew memento from his vest,
And sly on Donald's tartan laid
A shred to match his shortened plaid!

"Voila! morbleu — whoop! eh?"— he cried,
 But laughed with Donald, his traitor guide
  That fearful night! ... That shred he kept,—
  Torn from the plaid when Donald leapt
Into the jungle, terrified!
— Then Osseolo, shy and meek,
Drew near — a tear upon his cheek?—
And placed in Eben's coat of blue
A withered tuft of faded hue,
Dead leaves. . . .

    Dead loves!—that told a tale.
  Ah! none save Onnalinda knew
   What meant those flowers, or where they grew,
The daffodil and daisy pale!

XXIX

RONALD AND GLINTING STAR.

Now silent stood each warrior band
　As Onnalinda smiling went
And kissed The Star, and pressed her hand
　And led her close to Ronald Kent;
And in his hand she softly laid
　The trembling hand of Glinting Star!
　. . . Plaudits arose from near and far
For Ronald and the Algonquin maid!
— Said Kawanute in pleasant glee,
Half earnest and half raillery:
"Swifter and keener woman's glance
Than Saxon's rifle or his lance!
You boast of white man's strategy
Then captive fall to her dark eye! —
'T is well too warm a heart is hers
To tomahawk her prisoners!"

———

With merry greetings were they wed,
　And hailed with plaudits near and far.
　— Now rose the chief, oracular
With wise and frequent pause, and said:

"My children. . . . Happy be you all. . . .
    Have but one path — new trails go by. . . .
New trails for fools in traps to fall —
    One path leads up to yonder sky."

He turned to Onnalinda meek,
    His hand lay gently on her head,
    And in a tremulous voice he said,
While tears fell down his war-worn cheek:

"Be happy, child! . . . Wherever you go
My poor old heart will follow you. . . .
What your sweet mother was to me
You to the noble Eben be.
. . . We meet up in the happy sky —
Be glad. . . .
              Be happy. . . .
                        Sweet, good-bye."

When all these dusky clans — the unhappy descendants of Ka-wanute — have vanished from our forests, they may at least be permitted to live in Romance and Song. No bard have they to harp their heroic deeds; no scribe for confuting the wretched calumnies cast upon them; THEY ARE SILENT. Under the guise of romance, and the glamour of fancy, some truths may steal into unwilling ears: the purity and amiability as well as the adroitness of Onnalinda; the fidelity, modesty, and the aptitude for culture of Glinting Star, are truthful characterisations. Of Oonak we can only say: the red race, too, has its Judas! In the noble Kawanute one could wish that the defamers of his race could recognise a character worthy of their emulation.

ADDENDA.

ONE ASH,
ROCHDALE.

Sep. 1. 94.

Dear Sir.

I have received & read your Poem "Onnalinda" with great interest & pleasure – there is life & beauty in it which I have much enjoyed. I thank you for giving me the opportunity of reading what you have written.

I have sympathy with your Indian people. but have no power to help them. Their case is one of great hardship – for they have been

and are

the victims of your wild western
population whose violence it is not
easy for your Gov't to control.

You have put down the cruelties
practised on the negro. Is it not
possible for the friends of the negro
to raise their voices in defence of
the Red men? You have seized
their land, - You occupy almost all
their country. Can you not give them
the security your laws give to your
white millions? If the good men
& women of the States make an
effort

for their benevolent purpose, I think
it would not fail.

Your Poem will excite sympathy,
& I ~~could~~ hope it will do something
to soften the fate of the Tribes whom
the White man has dispossessed.

Accept my thanks for your
kind remembrance of me, &
believe me very truly Yours

John Bright.

Mr. J. H. McNaughton
Caledonia
New York

Knebworth
11 July
1884

Sir,
    Pray accept my
thanks for the gift
of your volume

    I have read 'Onnabæda'
with attention and
pleasure, and without
stopping, till I had
finished it. The story
is in itself a very pretty
one — You have told
it

it with great animation
of movement and picturesque
of description – And I
congratulate you on
having invested with
interest a subject
that deserves it

Your Obedient Servant

[signature]

J. H. McNaughton
Caledonia
New York

EXTRACTS FROM REVIEWS.

Westminster Review.

" . . . . Onnalinda sustains its interest from first to last. Strange to say, the tale is the pleasanter reading for being in metre, and the reader is beguiled past many pitfalls in the shape of 'asides' by the silvery ring of the verse."

London Morning Post.

" . . . . The subject is in itself attractive, and affords room for much picturesque description. Of this the author has duly availed himself. Mr. McNaughton tells his story with animation, and weaves the loves of the charming Onnalinda and her English lover into a pleasing poem."

Illustrated London News.

" . . . . The author has proved that the American muse can sing with sweetness and with spirit, with feeling and with humour. Space forbids the quotation of passages which would testify of felicitous expression, picturesque description, animated scenes, impressive action."

The Whitehall Review (London).

" . . . . The mixture of fact and fiction is skilfully managed; the quaint fancifulness which invests metaphor with artistic grace is bright and spontaneous; the wild beauty of the locality is tellingly delineated; and the picturesque appearance and chivalrous characteristics of the *dramatis personæ* are charmingly described."

The Christian World (London).

" . . . . Onnalinda is a strikingly beautiful romance. The story is told in a very fascinating manner — with a vivacity that never lags or fails from the first page to the last. We predict that all who make its acquaintance will accord to Mr. McNaughton their admiration and gratitude."

The Scottish Review.

" . . . . Mr. McNaughton's spirited appeal on behalf of the Red Indians is one in which every right thinking person will heartily sympathize. . . . The story is told with spirit and vigour, and the versification has force and power."

London Literary World.

" . . . . It is a poetic romance full of exciting and agreeable interest. The progressive nature of the poem is an important element in its enjoyment; one has not long to wait for the development of the story. . . . We have not read a poetic romance of its aim and length for many a day and year which takes our fancy more completely."